T0351463

World-Changing Rage

THE GERMAN LIST

World-Changing Rage

NEWS OF THE ANTIPODEANS

GEORG BASELITZ

ALEXANDER KLUGE

Assisted by Thomas Combrink

TRANSLATED BY

KATY DERBYSHIRE

LONDON NEW YORK CALCUTTA

This publication was supported by a grant from the Goethe-Institut, India.

Seagull Books, 2019

Originally published as Georg Baselitz, Alexander Kluge, *Welt-verändernder Zorn*. © Suhrkamp Verlag, Berlin, 2017. All rights reserved and controlled through Suhrkamp Verlag Berlin

English translation © Katy Derbyshire, 2019

First published in English by Seagull Books, 2019

ISBN 978 0 8574 2 657 4

British Library Cataloguing-in-Publication Data
A catalogue record for this book is available from the British Library

Typeset and designed by Seagull Books, Calcutta, India
Printed and bound by Hyam Enterprises, Calcutta, India

World-Changing Rage

B.VII 015

1

HOW THE WORLD CAME UNDER THREAT

MASKS OF RAGE

ALL ELEMENTS WERE AIMING AT CONTRADICTION

ODYSSEYS OF RAGE

HOKUSAI, THE ANTIPODEAN

How the world came under threat

One of the eight heavenly sins that the Japanese contrast god SUSANOO committed (he rules over strife and rage between earth and water, earthquakes and spring tides), was the REVERSE DESECRATION OF THE HIDE OF A HORSE. The scandalous god flayed the skin of the sun's trusty steed, cast the hide into the workroom of the weaver women who made fabrics for Amaterasu, the sun queen, and gave one of the women such a shock that she 'stabbed herself in the vagina with her shuttle and died'. At that moment, the otherwise most patient Amaterasu could not control her fury. She could not bear the weaver woman's scream, her shock. She ensconced herself inside a cave. The world was dark.

Overcoming the flush of rage via the diaphragm

The gods waited outside the cave for the sun to one day emerge again. A minor goddess by the name of Ame no Uzume, already elderly, comparable to a low mountain range worn down by weather (sunken, retaining barely any hills and revealed only to the excavating geologist), fell into a kind of trance due to the long wait in the dark outside the cave. She exposed her genitals and her meagre breasts and began to dance. The gods burst out laughing. Their tremendous laughter, nothing but contractions of the diaphragm, aroused the goddess Amaterasu's curiosity in her hiding place. She opened the entrance to the cave and looked outside. A minor god named 'Man of the Strong Hand of the Heavens' was standing near the entrance. He pulled the sun out of the cave. Ame no Futotama, a demon, actually an impostor among the gods, immediately tied a rope across the entrance. And so Amaterasu was prevented from returning to the cave. We Japanese owe the preservation of the world to the rather accidental humour of the ugly old goddess' performance, a world that almost perished as the result of a concentration of rage and fury, a congestion of anger.

The masses of the earth

Countless Japanese deities were originally identical to land masses. When the Japanese isles split off from the subcontinent, which bolted from the supercontinent Pangaea like a fleeing ship, the goddess Amaterasu was granted the sun and the planets. Also the stars, yet not the starry night.

The godhead is a river
flowed back into itself.

This goddess' brother, Susanoo, received dominion over the sea and the earth, in the places where war is waged. He is a saboteur. He considers the division between land and sea unjust, is eternally at odds with his sister.

Thus, one cause of the fury of the seas and the earthquakes that afflict the islands can be sought in the antagonistic division of the earth: in the privileging of the sun over the night side contained in the heavens (which has no god at all) and the rancour with which the sea and the cliffs ram one another. What god wants only to rule over strife?

'The Ecstasy of Things'

Master Hokusai looks naked in this drawing. Hand and foot are neighbours. Fearful siblings. His face a death mask.

To ease the pain, there are dots added where acupuncture might be applied, but the dots are slightly to one side of the places where the treatment would be effective. Not a good day.

The European ghost on the facing page, to which Hokusai is pointing: likewise a summation of dots, between which there are countless links. Maps of the spirit. One dot is composed of an unending number of individual dots. INFINITESIMAL. All the way down to nothing? There is no nothing in the dot. Uncountable? 'Innumerable.'

Both drawings contain a clever deception. The master's appearance is a masquerade. Nor is his European opposite a ghost—it is dancing. To the QUEST FOR HAPPINESS, which is inherent to us and a reliable pilot in unfamiliar territory, we must add a SECOND FORCE: the pursuit of COUNTER-HAPPINESS. That is, says Gottfried Benn, the mind. Only both types of happiness together link the Far East and the Occident. The dancing ghost sets one of its stampers (its muscular legs) in motion towards SKIN HAPPINESS. The other strives for GRIP. In truth, however, the man is concerned with EAR HAPPINESS; a sound is making him dance. It is his musical leg. No freedom without a quantum of counterhappiness.

No singing floats on the empty air

Masks of rage

We won't always find rage under its own name. Just as neither Master Hokusai nor Hölderlin responded to a single name. A dragon, a young heroine already grasped in its claws, was disappointed when it tasted with its greedy mouth and found nothing but empty skin. So it is with the names of great spirits. Tremendous rage dissolves to the southeast of the Harz Mountains, breaks down into collective efficiency. At the beginning was fury, when miners and peasants were burnt, their limbs torn, and they were killed for their revolt against the Count. They moaned in the last of their rage. That rage lived on as the skill with which their great-grandsons (all employed at vehicle-repair shops and filling stations), one night in May 1940, opened up 500 metres of the frontline in France and pierced through with their panzers all the way to the Channel. Out of reach for every 'superior', be he foe or friend. The spawn of fury frozen for centuries as a seed in these soldiers was still in effect on their return from Russia. In any case, it was more effective than the field telephones, with the aid of which a scattered, disjointed and demoralized troop of 300,000 men, the 1st Panzer Army, would never have been able to communicate on their breakout. Whereas they actually managed to find their way together though the furious nervousness planted in their souls (like mitochondria in a cell, by that point 417 years old, passed down through all family disputes). Thus, 'degenerate' rage and fury led them safely home.

All elements were aiming at contradiction
and yet moved unintentionally towards harmony

How would you interpret the facial expression in the picture at the bottom of page 7? This was what Gesine Mückert, who had visited the exhibition twice already, asked her male companion. The man was 'lissom'. He occasionally appealed to her; they had been living in shared quarters for eight months by that point (the equivalent to eight years of a traditional nineteenth-century marriage). 'Surly,' was her companion's answer. They were both secretly intending to separate in the near future.

What do you say to the picture Hokusai's finger is pointing at? (Gesine pointed at page 6.) The man, who had studied art history and sociology, saw the purposefulness of Hokusai's finger, its energy, as signs of a new 'type around 1600'. The new type, he said, arises 'with the emergence of bourgeois consciousness'. In Edo? Hence the spade at the bottom right of page 6? It is a question of 'confidence, based on the concept of labour'. Gesine was not convinced by her companion's means of expression. And the type is new? Even though humanity has always laboured? Now, though, in 1842 (the time in which Hokusai was alive), Gesine's partner answered, it takes place with hope on the horizon.

The couple debating the sketch came from central Germany. The man in the picture has a droopy dick, Gesine said. He needs his strength for construction, said her partner. The house is already built. Gesine's soon-to-be-ex-boyfriend pointed at the depicted man's groin. The new type has nice wavy hair, said Gesine. And the lady's shoes he's wearing go nicely. Is the hand part of a uniform? asked Gesine's companion. They came slightly closer again while they sipped at their coffee cups. That kind of thing often happens simply because people start talking to one another. Towards eleven o'clock, shortly after one another, they emptied their bowels. The bathrooms in the art palace were clean and well-kept. For a moment, Gesine contemplated the idea of returning to them, locking themselves into one of the cubicles and making up.

How should Hokusai's gaze be understood? Surely not as a critique of sensuality. The very opposite: as a command to remove all forms of indifference. The way one smashes crockery in the seventh year of a well-run marriage and comes closer to the other even while clearing up the 'damage'.

The allegedly original couple

We 'isolated individuals', we 'indivisibles' can still choose the root from which we want to originate. From Adam's rib or Eve's. Willi Hanskotte was determined not to be descended from Adam. He did not like himself as a fighter continuing the world's history as a slaughterhouse in all eternity. In the event of a rebirth, he wanted to be a creature he could stand to be around. Hence his robust avowal that he stemmed from Eve's rib.

Hokusai, however, hints at the possibility—in his *One Hundred Poems Explained by the Nurse*—that Adam and Eve were not the source of all humankind. There were very old creatures, during the transition from *homo erectus* to *homo sapiens*, who never crossed the garden of paradise—which was merely a zone between four rivers and the founding site of earlier cities in Mesopotamia, one of several centres of human evolution. Just as the central perspective was not reality, a couple in that garden of paradise were not held to be the origin of the Japanese. We can tell by the master's energetic gesture that this is not merely a suspicion but a certainty for him. Not even the connection of man and woman was imperative for the origin of humanity. Why did wit originate from the ribs? Why could a hero not just as well have emerged from the liver or the skin of the earthly queen Eve? Possibly, the original inhabitants of the Japanese isles not only came about without Adam and Eve but also out of entirely different limbs or innards or outer parts of an ancestor, travelled there from Africa. If not even born of gods! he tells us.

Couple-forming originates from the bygone paradise. From which type of twin, Hokusai asks, does the controversy arise? 'Beauty rears her ugly head.'

5 VII

6 156 あ.

Odysseys of rage

Rage changes the world. Something has been taken away from me. I respond with fury.

Thus, the fury of the peasants, the weavers, the cavalry horses in the machine-gun fire, the pain over the division of Poland, over the loss of German Alsace, the rage of the workers in the factories of the nineteenth century, must suffice to trigger a revolution in central Germany in 1923. That was the opinion of the theoretician Karl Korsch. That fury, however, where it could be proved in the first place, proved to be a volatile raw material, akin to a gas. Blown on the wind. Impossible to hold onto. Only amalgamated with National Socialist organization, the authoritarian administrative hand, melded with resentments, did that rage seem conservable, summonable, possibly dirigible. Impossible to recognize in this form by the furious themselves. Thus, this material, to the horror of critical minds, was not a material suitable for revolutionizing but easy to convert into MOTORIZED MOTION.

Obergruppenführer von dem Bach-Zelewski had to have his bowel emptied by hand. His irritated conscience, which his brain had commanded to quieten down, had caused recurring haemorrhoids. One of his bodily organs stubbornly refused to go on. Rage, entrenched against the ego in the bowel. Wildly fluorescing thumos. Practically incurable. Reich Physician SS Dr Rasch got stuck in day after day, with great patience but little success, to the backside of the locally anaesthetized commander.

The Queen of Shamakhi. A 1904 Japanese-Russian encounter.

A Russian fantasy. Alexander Pushkin told the story of a cockerel that warns the Russian empire whenever it is in danger by crowing three times. Years later, the story became an opera: the aged tsar must set out to wage war in the Far East, for the cock has crowed three times. There in the East, he faces the enchanting queen of Shamakhi, as the dawn. Instead of warring, the two of them marry. The young beauty rules over the tsar and thus over the country. The tsar dies of a bite from the cockerel.

Rage cut

In fencing, the line through which the blow is to pass is called THE RAGE CUT. It has an equivalent line on the palm of the fencer's hand with the name 'the sister of the heart line'. In the rare cases in which the two lines cross (over which the fencer has no control), the weapon cuts through every opponent's cover.

'Sparks of tears with the courage of rage'

Iracundia. Irascibility = standing fury. 'FURIOUS: like a tiger's heart.' A flush of rage on a face, in contrast, is a sign of strong emotion. Also: rays of fury. 'Fury's rage and love / Baited desperately on another / Both with eyes full of tears.'

A man in Bielefeld, after animated research on the Internet, arrived at the conclusion that all compounds of the German word ZORN (FURY/RAGE) were less commonly used expressions. During the very night on which he had finished his essay on the subject, he was overcome by doubt. He got up several times, not to urinate but to write down sentences that pursued him like wolves of love. No 'rampart of thoughts' rescued him from the words fury and rage, words containing a cage of beasts thirsting for freedom, burning with anger, confused and scenic beasts. More and more new formulations, series of words beginning or ending with fury and rage or bearing their signs in their middle, raced through the sleepless man's head.

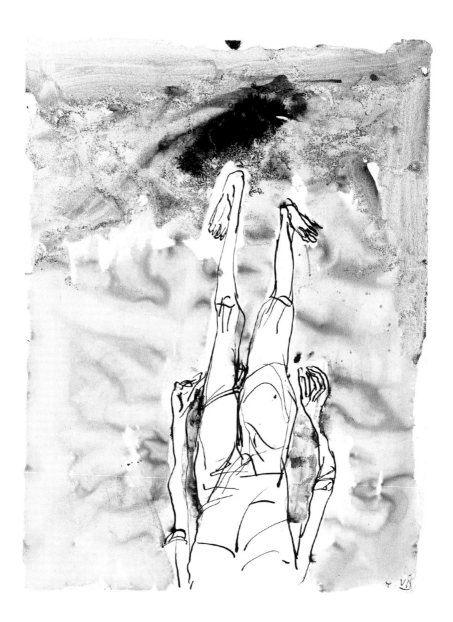

Snow over Venice

Snow fell upon the city in thick flakes. Still icy only hours ago, now it was too warm for the flakes to settle on the roofs of the palazzi. The lagoon's green water quickly consumed the snow.

It was not Arctic snow. This snow over Venice came from Africa. Cold rage had risen in the mountainous zone, in which French military engineers, trained as panel beaters, amateurs with regard to toxic gas, sprayed their canisters into caves where they suspected Tuareg rebels. The wailing laments of the women whose husbands they had killed preyed on their ears all night long, robbed France's tired soldiers of their sleep. Out of the death caves, however, fury rose to the skies and settled beneath the stratosphere. It migrated northwards as a cold cloud, ending up above the lagoon city, a miraculous weather phenomenon. A state of mind that only came back into contact with the surface of the earth in the millennial city, like tears transformed into rain. Cold rage. The snow's thaw an illusion.

Hokusai, the Antipodean

He is poised there in his skin. He has given himself nineteen names. His finger points westwards. In him and around him the spider's web of a lively mind. A counterpart in the Ore Mountains might tread on his skull. But no one does so. All respect the master. 'Tell me what your name is, and I'll know what you are called.' This saying from Halberstadt, intended as a joke, can't harm the master. 'What a sloppy thing the SELF can be.'

'56 Bv

Master Hokusai's harp

Master Hokusai refers to the Western ghost with sarcasm: the human individual, caged in his intentions. A cut like an operation wound, vertical, divides the ghost (page 38). In addition to the horizontal division that all people have. At the top the breath, the noble facial expressions, the only thing protruding from the suit naked (with a little neck)—that is the SACRED TOP HALF. The MALTREATED BOTTOM HALF: the walking legs' skeins of muscle, the intestinal loops, the spermatic cords. The bottom half must labour.

In the horizontal intermediate zone, the diaphragm. That is the harp upon which Master Hokusai likes to play. Laughter in Japan is a likeness of the constant fateful earthquakes, impossible to prevent and which plunge the islands into commotion.

2

THE LONG JOURNEY FROM 'ME' TO THE FAR EAST

MADAME BUTTERFLY'S SON

LONGER THAN TEN MILLENNIA

HOW A FORMERLY YOUNG IMPERIAL GENERAL
  WAS STILL DEFENDING HIS POSITION IN 1993

WHEN I WAS NINE YEARS OLD, JAPAN CONSISTED FOR ME OF A PUZZLING PROPAGANDA IMAGE. THE THIRD REICH PROPAGANDISTS WERE AMBIVALENT TOWARDS JAPAN. THE SOLDERS AND BATTLESHIPS OF THE FARAWAY, NON-ARYAN NATION WERE SEEN AS EXEMPLARY. BUT AS EARLY AS MARCH 1942, A DEMARCATION LINE WAS DRAWN BETWEEN THE GERMAN AND THE JAPANESE SECTORS (IN THE EVENT OF THEM CONQUERING THE WORLD TOGETHER). THE LINE CUT THROUGH INDIA. WE COULD TRACE IT IN OUR SCHOOL ATLAS.

I KNOW MORE ABOUT THE MOON THAN ABOUT THOSE DISTANT ISLANDS IN THE EAST. I DO HAVE A PRECISE REASON, HOWEVER, FOR FEELING DRIVEN TO WRITE ABOUT JAPAN WITH SUCH A FOOLISH ENDOWMENT OF EXPERIENCE. IT IS TO DO WITH ONE OF MY STRONGEST EARLY IMPRESSIONS AT THE CINEMA.

A lasting first impression of 'Japan'

In the autumn of 1941, time began to run out for me. In my first year at the cathedral grammar school at which I had been enrolled since Easter, I was having trouble keeping up. The tutoring my mother had arranged immediately after the disasters of the first few weeks would only help in the long term. In those fast-paced times, the Capitol cinema was showing *Premiere der Butterfly*, a German-Italian coproduction. The film is set in the days immediately after the premiere of Puccini's blockbuster opera *Madame Butterfly*, in the year 1904 (four years before my mother was born).

The plot—before the singer Rosi Belloni (Maria Cebotari) can inform her fiancé, the music student Harry Peters (Fosco Giachetti), that she is expecting his child, he tells her he has got a booking in America. For the sake of his future, Rosi advises him to take the offer. Years pass, in which Rosi never hears from Harry. She raises her child and matures into a great artist. At her request, the premiere of Puccini's new opera *Butterfly* is moved to La Scala in Milan. Among the guests is the conductor of the Metropolitan Opera. Rosi recognizes him as Harry. She learns he is now married. Aside from that, she realizes he has come to see not her but the opera. Only now does Rosi see the remarkable similarity between her personal fate and the opera's plot. Hence, she plays her part with distressing intensity (the film features close-ups of the lovers in the Japanese wooden house in the opera's first act). Not a word of rebuke crosses Rosi's lips. FROM NOW ON SHE BELONGS ENTIRELY TO HER ART AND HER CHILD.

'Harakiri'

Theodor W. Adorno called Fritz Lang his 'brother in kitsch', not without affection. It was not meant to be derogatory, he responded to my query. Otherwise, he added, he wouldn't have spoken of a *brother*. He meant by it a certain audacity, brutality or lack of concern with which Lang—because it was part of the film business—cut back material and operatic plots for the benefit of the audience and his directing. Adorno's statement referred to a 1919 silent movie with the title *Harakiri*, Lang's 'second film in the Decla world class' made in Berlin.

The father of a young Japanese woman by the film name of O-Take-San, a merchant straight out of a Lessing drama, returns from Europe to Nagasaki and showers his beloved daughter with gifts, among them costume jewellery and a teddy bear from London. The village priest, the so-called *bonze*, keeper of the Yoshiwara shrine, sees the souvenirs from afar as a contamination and a religious violation. The father commits harakiri due to his accusations. The daughter, however, is to serve the priest as a 'sub-priestess'. In the 'sacred garden of Buddha', she meets a Dutch naval officer. They enter into a temporary marriage in the Japanese tradition, a 'union of 999 years'. The Dutchman has been using O-Take-San, however. For a long time, he sends no news from Holland. Years later, he returns to Japan, accompanied by a European wife, upon which the exotic beauty casts herself on her father's sword.

The aim of the plot, as Adorno commented, was the avoidance of a copyright collision with Puccini's original material. A large part of the opera's meaning and emotionally comprehensible situations were sacrificed to this concern.

Lang concentrated instead on parallel montages. With no relation to the plot, we see a group of dungeon masters in the temple and watch the seducers' collective in the Dutch naval club. The temple interior where the religious dungeon masters were housed was dark brown, the teahouse and the officers' mess bright yellow. (Fassbinder imitated this colouring method in his last films, although they were no longer made in black and white.)

151 B.

As an experienced tenor . . .

As an experienced tenor, I would like to take a stand against the common vilification of Pinkerton in Puccini's *Madame Butterfly*, the character I embody. One can of course claim that Puccini arranged the part so that the audience cannot forgive the tenor for the death of the soprano at the end of the play. That is not the situation in the first act, however, on which my role as a singer is primarily based. There is no denying a certain warmth to my role, particularly my appearance during the love duet. I put that cordiality into my voice, at any rate.

I see the American naval officer I embody as a commander of a warship. He becomes involved with a lady from a once-powerful Japanese aristocratic line. She was brokered to him professionally, as a *hetaere* in the ancient Greek sense, so to speak. He spends his weeks on leave with her. He regards the 'mock marriage' as a common local ritual. He has no guilty conscience when he returns to service and the USA.

He does not learn that the young woman fell pregnant until the time between the second and third acts, at the earliest. In the meantime in the USA, he has married into a Protestant family that furthers his career. His wife Kate cannot have children. It is not the fault of the tenor that she, having found out about her husband's pre-marital offspring, has the idea of adopting Butterfly's child, partly to strengthen their marriage of convenience, and travels to Nagasaki with her husband for that purpose. Due to my emotional involvement with the part of Pinkerton (I have sung the role 386 times now, note for note), I am convinced that the tangle of fate, the Japanese woman's tragic self-aggression, is based on a misunderstanding between two cultures, a CLASH. At no time did this woman accept the status of a commercial service she felt forced into performing due to her father's death and the accompanying loss of fortune. She never understood what happened to her. She does not possess a 'capitalist soul'. The tenor was raised very differently. I see him as a lively, mercurial primate who considers himself a fortunate prince, an exponent of a modern naval fleet. What drives him and what flows melodiously from my throat is a spirit of taking and accepting advantage, to which all my senses submit, as does a kind of registering bookkeeping in my code of honour ('Don't miss a chance to climb the ranks, don't let any rival leave you behind.'). I would also like to point out that the mock marriage in the first act and the promises of which the tenor sings took place under the influence of alcohol, intensified by the rush of anticipation of love. Two souls come together here; their minds misunderstand each other but their senses are united. Before any international court of arbitration, occupied by equal numbers of Japanese and Americans, Pinkerton would be found not guilty. Nor is he unfaithful, though he appears reckless by nature, as he remains true to himself at all times.

He dies with honour
who cannot live with honour.

This message, left by the young Japanese woman for Pinkerton, necessarily alienates me, the tenor. I play that at this point in the drama by stumbling. I consider it an atavistic rule that goes against the sensual joy of my vocals.

Madame Butterfly's son

They say the son of the beautiful Madame Butterfly, taken from her household after her death and raised by his American father, a naval officer, and his wife (an heiress from Boston), started a career at the age of 17 at the Annapolis naval academy. Later, the young man married into a butcher's family in Chicago.

In 1943, this boy is then (aged 39) said to have distinguished himself in the night-time attack on the wooden suburbs of Tokyo. He led the scout planes that set the marks for the bombers, showing them precisely where to cast their explosives. In the attack, the wooden house ('the bungalow') in which the love story took place was burnt to the ground.

We can rule out that anything made of wood remained standing in that sub-prefecture of Tokyo to which Madame Butterfly's home belonged. The fire raged for three days and three nights. According to Irmi Downsland, who looked into the matter, the walls without which that intimate hour between the naval officer and the Japanese woman would not have taken place, wood from 1904, were reliably DESTROYED. There is no proof of that supposition, however, said a mail from the Paris-based researcher Gabriele W., with whom Irmi corresponded. At the very least, she wrote, Irmi should note that the proficient navigation officer, 'made of strong stuff', who apparently flew a Mosquito bomber plane 'also made of wood', had survived the events of 1944 and returned to Nebraska in one piece after the offensive. That showed, she wrote, that a subsequent nothing, which was never complete, could not retroactively reset a former SOMETHING completely to zero. To which Irmi responded 'by return of post' (in fact 'computer-compatibly'): SUPERSTITION!

A more fortunate cousin of Madame Butterfly

In only the second semester of her degree at an art academy in southern Germany, the daughter of a brewery owner (with latifundia in Bavaria, and in the Czech Republic) met and fell in love with a Japanese man. This man was a member of the academy's technical crew and had come to Germany (from a poor, landless family near Osaka) as an electrician. In the meantime, the mixed-ethnic couple have two beautiful children, a boy and a younger girl. Today, they're having breakfast in a cafe.

The young blonde woman is wearing a blue skirt and, in strong contrast, a blood-red scarf wrapped three-hands' width around her neck, sumptuous décor. Her Buddha in cord trousers is at the head of the table, slightly stiff. The children are both a bit of a handful, and have used the signs outside the cafe with the special offers written on them to build a hut.

The man has 'practical', slightly inelegant, almost technical movements. When they get up to leave, he lifts his daughter onto his back with a strong hand and then wraps her around his belly. She bends her young body accordingly, as though it were a circus act. The four of them are part of no aristocracy, they are not citizens of the same land, their social backgrounds are different, they belong to none of the familiar target groups, they dress and move differently, have differing skin colours and differing allergies. All that has mixed in their children. Evidently without conflicts.

Recently, the four of them saw MADAME BUTTERFLY at the Easter Festival in Salzburg, in a conventional staging in Italian. The US naval officer central to the opera's plot was sung by a Japanese tenor. The role of the Japanese woman seduced and then abandoned by him, with the traditional name of 'Butterfly', was played by a singer from Birmingham who looked like an heiress to the English aristocracy in the nineteenth century.

The happy holidaymakers, sitting in good seats in the Festspielhaus (the young woman's account always kept topped up by her brewery-owning father), laughed at the performance. They were not in the mood for tragedy.

Longer than ten millennia

For longer than ten millennia, the Jōmon elites lived in Japan as collectors of fine lacquer paintings and jade objects. And yet as a hunter-gatherer society. So impassioned, perfected and intelligent at hunting, gathering and fishing that the generations did not think to change their social contract, their relationships to one another or to nature. They possessed monumental cult sites, suited for highly imaginative festivals but not for habitation. Not until 300 BCE did husbandry break into the territory in which the Jōmon tribes lived. No bronze and no iron age. These occurred only late, imported.

Then, in 1904, the victory over Russia with metal cannons and steel ships. Navigation, discipline in the troops, precision of the artillery. Their mathematical skill still follows the mental rhythm of the Jōmon elites. A Japanese bank has bought up and fenced in an excavation area in the north of Hokkaido where archaeological finds and cult sites occur en masse. A nature park is to be built there, not for contemporary Japanese nature but for a nature of eleven thousand years ago. Manufacture of pristine nature and respect for the ancestors in the interest of the brand image of the highly credit-worthy, internationally networked bank, which holds 12 per cent of the countervalue of its lendings as assets in its safes and balances.

3. VIII 0.15

5. VII. 015

How a formerly young imperial general was still defending his position in 1993

1

He was bitterly old. His world had ended twice: through the Japanese defeat in 1945 and through a company collapse in 1956. Now he was vice president of a major corporation in Tokyo. He was of a mind to defend this third world, his last rank, blindly.

His own flesh was devouring him from within. Cancer of the oesophagus, inoperable. Establishing that was no effort. What was laborious was the procedure of taking him secretly to the clinic for out-patient treatment without raising suspicions in the company. No one was entitled to ask questions of him, the vice president.

2

As far as the world is concerned, he runs the international department of a global corporation. The foreign investments are all in deficit. He doesn't understand the mechanisms. Ambitious young subordinates claim to understand what goes on in the NEW ECONOMY. In formal meetings, they are allowed to share their views only if he expressly asks them. He avoids such meetings.

What practical work does he do at the office? He endures. He holds up 'progress'. In fact, however, he also prevents the decisive attack on his authority that would take place immediately if he were to give up a grain of his power.

For weeks he has been sitting in his office from five in the morning, barricaded in. The sun rises in the east of the island; he can't sleep. He is fed by transfusion. On a daily basis, before morning comes, trusted retainers transport him to the 56th floor of the skyscraper in the centre of Tokyo and instal him on a special chair in his office. Here, within arm's reach of telephones and classic writing equipment, he maintains his position until midnight, making him the first and last man in the building.

3

The blinds are down. Outer offices protect the old man. One of his secretaries is in fact an oncologist. There is no way to hold up the passage of time leading to his death and the end of his role as vice president. He will do nothing—just as he did nothing as a general of the Japanese emperor's military engineers in 1945—to actively precipitate his demise.

As an engineer general, he conquered islands for the emperor. That came to an end. When his comrades founded industries, a fellow fighter who had employed him—chief of plant security, a major in the Pacific island battles—dragged him down with him. Matsumoto had commanded Tokyo's military police in the final struggle for Japan, and now he failed terribly, had taken bribes. That was his second demise.

He re-climbed the company ranks to Position No. 3, which he now occupies. He loses grip on reality; he and several colleagues ranked below him, his retinue. They would topple if he toppled. He is too old to study ways out. The solution is to regard that which purports to be the NEW REALITY as unreality.

4

His internal membrane, the piece of skin between his stomach and his throat that he's never seen but which brought him in one piece through all the battles of the Second World War, the hardships of 1947, through conferences and decisive moments, has been taken away from him. A piece of his stomach wall was sewn onto the membranes of his pharynx. He can't swallow, can only speak to a limited extent. The little he's learnt to say is sufficient to keep important telephone callers in conversation.

As the language courses that enable him to offer brief questions or replies in a reedy tone could only take place at night but he could not leave his office for longer than a day, there was little opportunity to learn to use his new body and voice after the operation. There would be little point, in any case, due to the progress the evil is inscribing on his new skin.

There is a blackmailer on the sixth floor. He claims to know something about the destruction inside the powerful man's body. His information (or 'suspicion') is false. He refers to the vice president having a brain tumour, and sends secret messages on the matter. The sixth floor is under the command of Sensu Idikai, an opponent of the vice president for decades. The superior power of No. 3 does not extend to these depths. It would be intercepted by the personnel department and would lead to enquiries as soon as he tried to cause harm to the blackmailer.

And so he operates with promotions. The blackmailer's entire network is brought into the international department, crippling his coterie entirely.

5

A porter might bump into him and he'd fall. Physically incapable of defence. He could destroy anyone in his department for their entire career; indeed, he could kill them due to his power to shame them before all the others by demoting them.

On the other hand, he no longer has control over his back muscles. He sits bent, his chest resting against his desk. His sternum, the doctors say, is of a crumbly consistency and might shatter at any moment.

How does this powerful man keep his desire in balance? Every individual needs a quantum of desire so as to somehow walk the path to death. He manages to gain desire by remembering shame he has avoided in the past. That feeling can be rationed when a person has time. One needs only loneliness and an absence of disruptions.

26.VII.015

3

THE FLEET HAD RECEIVED A BRITISH EDUCATION

WERE GREAT MASSES OF RAGE BEARERS ON BOARD?

SUBMERSIBLE WORKBENCH

A ROBINSON OF THE SOUTH PACIFIC

WE ALL ACTED HERE 'AS THOUGH THERE WERE
A POINT TO IT'

The fleet had received a British education

In the Japanese admiralty, the realists had the upper hand. The fleet had received a British education. The conduct of the war had been coordinated with a number of counterparts in the German navy for the period January–September 1942. Only within this window, Admiral-in-Chief Yamamoto assumed, was a positive outcome of the war conceivable for Japan (and within limits, provided a certain judiciousness could be assumed there, for Germany as well). That spring, the Japanese fleet moved out its eight aircraft carriers, both its super-battleships and countless escort vessels, sending them past Ceylon and Madagascar towards the Red Sea. Had they succeeded in reaching Suez and linking up there with the Afrikakorps, the world would have been cut in two. The Axis powers would have had control of the Arabs' oil. American historians in Harvard and Stanford have documented this project, aiming for a negotiated peace with the USA after a surprising military coup, under the term GRAND DESIGN.

After the sinking of the British battleships *Prince of Wales* and *Hood* and the aircraft carrier *Hermes,* there was nothing to prevent the imperial fleet from reaching the Suez Canal. For Rommel's Swabian panzer operators, the phantasmagoria of physically encountering their Far Eastern allies would have been reason enough to cross the few hundred kilometres past Cairo to Port Said. In war, everything is a matter of what can be imagined. Yamamoto's staff sketched out conditions for an agreed peace: a free hand in one half of China and participation in the oil sources in southeast Asia. However, during the days in which the keels of the imperial fleet made their way through the western Indian Ocean, an imperial conference took place in Tokyo. Generals of the Japanese ground forces, caught up in their dogged progress towards China, pressed the navy representatives into a minority. The fleet was ordered back to the homeland. Australia was to be occupied. Shortly later, the imperial fleet sailed to its destruction at Midway.

Were great masses of rage bearers on board?

The only trace of wood in the officers' cabins. Everything else made of steel. Thus the six aircraft carriers headed for the Red Sea. With the same target: cruisers, destroyers, minesweepers. Submarines well ahead. That was the IMPERIAL COMBINED FLEET OF JAPAN. Where there heroes inside those ships? World-changing men of rage? The Japanese commanders would have liked to see it that way. Artists were busily drawing the seamen for the day of their victory.

In fact, the inmates of those steel behemoths were rice farmers. Disguised in the uniforms of the navy. With no opportunity to perform anything other than daily activities, beginning with regular bowel movements. The ships, oil-fired, moved 'as if of their own accord' through the blue water of the Indian Ocean. Not even the strong tailwind had a noteworthy influence on the fleet's speed. Through their binoculars, the navigators kept an eye out that none of the ships disrupted the neat parade order, be it by accelerating or delaying. Absolutely contrary to the laws of war and the intractable ocean, which whirl everything out of place.

Thus, it was not a CONCENTRATED MOTIF crossing the waves, though this advance might have decided the course of the war—providing it had still been a war of defence at that point, as originally planned, with the goal of a negotiated solution to the Pacific conflicts. The sister of fury: sagacity. Born out of original rage and fury as from a rib, then transformed into proportion and scouting attention. Now, the sister faced her brother Fury: in the mind of the commander of the Combined

Fleet, Yamamoto. The vessel of his soul held very little rage, perhaps 8 to 12 per cent, all the rest flooded with sagacity. Yet this one man could not be everywhere. While he was leading the warships at sea, his authority was lacking at the imperial liaison conference in Tokyo. Absolute radio silence between the two locations.

Had the fleet only been 400 kilometres further ahead, the Arabian oilrigs would have been on the starboard side. Transformed by the desperate Britons into torches, with towers of smoke touching the sky. Yet long extinguished again for the Japanese mental eye, and welling up with the JUICES OF THE EARTH, an energy source from the solar time 250 million years ago, as if preordained by the gods to provide for the Combined Fleet. That was the moment when betrayal prevailed, behind the backs of the rice farmers in the uniforms of maritime heroes and the sage monument placed on the bridge of the battleship *Yamato* in a smart white uniform: the betrayal of the original war plan, committed at the imperial liaison conference. The decision was an act of desperation. Yamamoto, had he been there, would have blown into such a conspiracy like a storm. He alone possessed the nonchalance and the 'braveness before the friend' to dash the aggressive pan-Asian conquest plan to the ground. The modern hero needs no war weapons; he decides the battles from the hills of budgets and committees.

'The body's seven cravings for buoyancy'

When the US SS-487 went down in the Timor Sea, a young navy cadet by the name of Harry from Oak Park, Illinois, which is where Hemingway came from too, had got hold of one of the last devices with which shipwrecked men can reach the surface from a submarine. Fished out of the water by the Japanese and taken to their flagship, the YAMATO, he was undergoing an interrogation when the battleship was completely destroyed by bombs and torpedoes and sank to the bottom of the sea. He was incarcerated between steel walls weakly lit by emergency lights. Still full of willpower. A ship's wall ruptured, and so Harry ended up in the open water and was drawn down to the depths.

How did he come to experience a whole human life after that? The reason for his rescue was the SEVEN FORCES OF BUOYANCY. They reside, in varying strength, in every individual.

The first force is that of the LUNGS. They possess a dogged will of their own. Even after the exhaustion of all their bearer's strength, after the loss of his will to survive, they insist on making it through to breathable oxygen, to the blue of the sky.

The second force of buoyancy was Harry's LEVITY. The jolly nature so valued by his comrades kept his muscles warm as he fought his way up the now-vertical steel corridors of the ship's interior. Then in the deep water. He was still treading water when his body lay calmly on the surface of the nocturnal sea in the dusky light of the stars. He would have been better off playing 'dead man'—it would have spared his energy.

The third force of buoyancy was his DISBELIEF. His mother had warmed her feverish child against her skin. Harry lacked the vision that death, masked as deep green water, might mean him. He refused desperation.

The fourth force of buoyancy was CONGESTED IMPROBABILITY. In invisible capsules, it slumbers in the veins of the brave. Ineptitude (he had never before swum to the surface from a depth of 80 metres) made his resistance against the water pressure less strong. That was the necessary dose of luck, because it slowed down his buoyancy so that the gas in his veins and cells did not explode through overly fast pressure alteration. No mind in the world could control fine-tuning like this.

The fifth force was the BRIGHT VOICES OF THE SIRENS. They did not lure the young man but propelled him upwards. They fired the fighter on with their songs. Had the maritime hero not been prepared for such a message in his inner self, he would have heard nothing and would surely have drowned. All seven forces of buoyancy must take effect *simultaneously*.

The sixth force consisted of a momentary HESITATION BY THE HAND OF GOD. One finger rests on the demise of the world. Yet there are interruptions in God's activities, or those of nature. This has saved many suicides and accident victims from death. No one can deliberately discover or make use of this moment of hesitation.

The seventh force came from the DISTANT FUTURE. A future offspring pulled his greedily kicking ancestor from the depths. The navy cadet had to be rescued, a wife found, a daughter conceived and this daughter had to give birth to this particular son, so that this boy of the future, a stocky fellow, could come to poor Harry's aid. This tracker dog from the future sent the drowning man speeding through the last 10 metres to the surface—an almost imperceptible force, a breath, a kind of wind, not measurable by devices (wind rarely finds its way under water). The procedure cannot be reproduced in experiments.

One further coincidence was required to rescue Harry—namely, that a Javanese fishing boat picked him up as he floated on the calm sea and he was thus not discovered by a Japanese patrol. Harry stayed six months in their village and helped with the harvest.

> Heaven has a long arm,
> if it is minded to save a man.

Submersible workbench

For the Japanese engineer, a submarine is not a fish. Just as a plane cannot be compared to a bird. If such machines start to 'sing', that announces their demise. I prefer to compare a submarine to a 'submersible workbench'. The surface of the sea is the table. The propellers protruding from the stern of the boat and the torpedo tubes at the stern and prow are the machine's weak points, however. They are not absolutely watertight; at high speeds, they tear the boat at its seams.

The deck, in contrast (not only the water surface) can be seen as a desk or table, floor space for the tower, the aerials, the artillery equipment, the structures for storing the dismountable seaplane. These installations *work*.

We crossed the Pacific with this table. We could have built underwater cities to the edges of the Mariana Trench with diggers and drills, attached to that table as additional weight. In fact, we successfully placed 'tents' on the bottom of the sea before Guadalcanal, structures for housing mechanical experts, in stationary submarines so to speak, in the underwater landscape, our underwater stronghold.

The idol that we Japanese engineers try to emulate goes by the name of INVULNERABILITY. Invulnerable are the inmates of our mobile workbenches as they cross the Pacific. They form an extreme threat to the usurping enemy. The more iron the enemy puts on the water, the more terrible our harvest will be.

Unheroic use of an engineered precision weapon

Japan's FIRST ASIAN BATTLE FLEET was ruled by engineers, as is well known. Battleships were a particular favourite of these engineers. They and the 6th Submarine Fleet, extreme opposites. On one side the battleships with their high masts, a GIGANTIC INDUSTRIAL INSTALLATION; the other side the submarines, a WEAPON OF ADVENTURE filled with elite consciousness.

The boats were piled high with new inventions: hydrogen paraffin torpedoes, the best torpedoes in the world. Batteries providing power US engineers could only dream of. The seaplane ready for assembly, carried by the submarine, extended the ship's rule of the sea, when used for reconnaissance purposes, by a perimeter of 400 kilometres. All the fleet's preparations were undertaken for the decisive battle. There could only be ONE of these, and it had to take place within the first year of the war.

At that time, the emperor ordered the submarines to be refitted for transporting supplies to the island of Guadalcanal. What shame! The valuable techniques of advanced combines, submersible, all-powerful, misused as 'pack horses for the army'! From the deciders of battle to transporters for food and ammunition!

They attempted to expel rice sacks from torpedo tubes. But the sacks burst open. They tried it with large biscuit tins, strapped to the surface of the boats, 6 metres in diameter. After that with cylindrical wooden containers. They broke as well. They were improvisations, not fitting tasks for engineers. Rice was tied down to the surface of the submarines in rubber sacks, ready to be unloaded near the beach. It emerged that the seawater seeped through the rubber. Later, a freight tube was developed. It resembled a flat landing vehicle. Two tons of such provisions could be stored on the deck of one of the highly specialized submarines, specifically designed for final battles. Powered by two torpedoes, a man sitting on top of one of the torpedoes steered the freight tube 2 nautical miles towards the coast. Had the engineers on Truk (who had no contact to the engineers in the harbours on the home front) had four years' time, they would have optimized such transport containers, a submarine transport weapon in itself. All they had to do was get the parcels off the submarine in one piece inside the diving lung.

In January 1943, twenty submarines were at sea, keeping the Japanese infantrymen on the island just about alive. What shame! No sight of a decisive battle! The boats could not show themselves anywhere on the seas. The torpedo tubes, all the hatches, were ruined by rice spelt. Though it went on another two years, the war was already lost.

No 'common present' among Antipodeans

Surrounded by dark forests where Serbian partisans lay in wait, a Japanologist from Kaiserslautern sat in a warm staff headquarters. Because he could write quickly, his job was to process leave applications and supplies lists. In his vicinity, his comrades died outside or were brutally mutilated.

He could tap his finger on the opposite side of the world in an atlas. Beneath that fingertip, 80,000 Japanese were currently victorious or dying. For the young Japanologist, a Wehrmacht lance corporal, however, 'seeking Japan with his soul' took him—due to the intensity of his thoughts—not to 1943 but to 1834. A more fortunate temporal territory than his present day.

A Robinson of the South Pacific

On his emperor's orders, a Japanese soldier held out on an island some distance from Rabaul. For fifteen years. Without news. He had prepared himself to repel a landing troop of US Marines, provided they were no more than thirty men, using his weapons, which he oiled every week. He had kept himself nourished on roots and fruit.

He had caught a lizard. Instead of a slave, which he wouldn't find. He had built a fence of bamboo poles around the lizard and he 'conversed' with it every day, like with another person, while the lizard snapped at him and never grew tame.

For years, not a ship on the horizons. Once, he drifted out a few miles onto the grey ocean on a raft in search of a neighbouring island. The walkie-talkie he possessed had given up the ghost some time ago.

In the fifteenth year, the haggard, bearded man was picked up by a coastal schooner from Java. He was returned to his homeland via the Japanese consulate. No one there had been waiting for him. He still possessed enough of the imperial discipline needed to survive in a men's boarding house. He felt more of a stranger in his 'homeland' than on his island where he'd had the illusion that his presence, his guard, was of use to his country. He wanted to be useful to others, create a place for himself in the world on which a man can stand. The space he inhabited in the boarding house was 2.1 metres in size, for himself and his belongings. The fatherland would have been glad to thank him, in view of the sensation his return provoked in the press. But what might such thanks consist of?

Disappointing arrival in East Asia

Germany ought to have had such Class XXI submarines in 1941! Twelve of them would have been capable of ruling the Indian Ocean. Now, in the early summer of 1945, one such vessel, loaded with rare metals, patent drawings set down in caskets and aid goods, arrived in a Japanese war harbour on Java. Unloading of the goods and handover to the Japanese authorities who no longer felt they were allies of the German Reich. Frosty negotiations over the acquisition of fuel. The diesel here was too viscous for the submarine's engines. Was there any other fuel? It had been a mistake to deliver the boat's cargo so quickly to the Japanese. It would have been better to leave the harbour the first night, submerge in the sound and negotiate from there with the authorities. Then they could only have counted on promises until the boat was back in the dock and being unloaded, though. After that, promises wouldn't have been kept. The frosty negotiations took their time. The German seamen had spent the long journey across the Indian Ocean anticipating steam baths and Japanese massages. They were emotionally starved. They were taken to a camp, guarded by Japanese military police. They didn't even have the rights of prisoners of war, because they weren't being held by enemies but in the captivity of disappointed allies.

Japanese engineers seized the abandoned submarine. At night, they came into the camp and tried to find out how it worked. Together, they could have looked for a large American aircraft carrier and sunk it with a few of the torpedoes they'd brought along. In that depressive atmosphere, however, there could be no more thought of cooperation.

Robinsonade in the ice

Two high-ranking SS and police officers, involved in murder campaigns and linked by friendship, were in the service of the German embassy in Tokyo in April 1945. The two friends had no wish to end up prisoners of the Allies (though the closure of the German embassy at an as-yet-undetermined time was unavoidable). They chartered a Japanese whaling ship, which took them to one of the Kerguelen Islands, an almost deserted French island in the very south of the South Pacific, covered in ice.

In the spring of 1945 they kept a calendar like Robinson Crusoe, having spent some weeks in the isolation of their tent. The whaler must already have reached its Japanese mother island. There was so little likelihood of ever getting away from their island, a territory of ice and scree, and thus attaining the company of others (even though those others would arrest them and punish them for their crimes), that they decided to shoot each other. Thus, one shot at the other. Between the shots, however, was a fraction of a second, so that one of the men was hit by a fatal bullet, the other not. The survivor lay severely wounded for several days as a 'remainder' in the shelter of the tent. After that, he considered himself sufficiently recovered to shoot himself (he had feared nothing more than an imprecise shot). No man can survive without the company of others.

Message across the dateline

Two radio operators still squatted in the rubble of the Japanese embassy on the edge of Berlin's Tiergarten park on the last day of April 1945. There were Russian snipers nearby. No glass left in the windows. Late that evening, they heard of Hitler's death by listening in to German radio communications (that was what they were trained for). It remained unclear for a while whether the Führer had been killed by enemy artillery fire, a putsch or his own hand. They translated the news into Japanese, encoded it and sent the text to Tokyo. The message reached the Tokyo headquarters at three in the morning. At that time, an airstrike on the city was about to begin, showering explosive and incendiary bombs. The message went unheeded for many hours. Between the radio message's dispatch in Berlin and reception in Japan lay the dateline.

1569.

Too late and by the wrong means

At the last minute, while Japan's surrender was under negotiation with the Allies, it was a handful of forceful officers who occupied the imperial palace along with the troops protecting Tokyo—that is, with battalions, vehicles and horses, generators for radio equipment and baggage train. They shot the commander of the palace guard. The emperor, however, whom the officers of the palace guard had hidden in the rambling grounds, evaded them. Without the emperor, the patriotic rebels could change nothing. And had they found him in his garden house, they could not have forced him into anything. He knew they would never shoot at the SUN. So what form might any force have taken? They knew nothing of the gramophone record on which the emperor's speech had been preserved. They might have been bristling with weapons, but they had no knowledge of audio technology. And so there was no option but seppuku. The soldiers brought in by the officers, lost in the palace grounds, marched back to their barracks. They were nothing but ruins. With artillery, of which they had plenty, they could not rid the world of a surrender document that no one could locate.

We all acted here 'as though there were a point to it'

The Japanese prime minister's face on the evening of 26 June 1945 mirrors his fatal exhaustion. Sleep refuses to come that night, for him and his staff. An old Japanese rule of thumb for sleep says: (1) no foe, no fear, peaceful place in my own 'property' (2) fall asleep (3) awake satisfied.

Anything else does not count as sleep, for the Japanese. Such an opportunity for sleep is not to be expected in the hour to hour and a half in which civil servants, liaison officers and ministers must wait by the telephones for a response to their urgent questions. I am writing this although my message has no addressee.

Surrender at an unusual point in time

The capture of the *last* Japanese soldier of the Second World War is a remarkable case. The Japanese lieutenant Onoda Hirō surrendered on the Filipino island of Lubang in March 1974, 29 years after the end of the war. He said he had heard the loudspeaker vehicles that had instructed him to give himself up (he was terrorizing the island with his combat unit from the jungle), as well as his own brother's voice telling him to surrender. He had come to the island, however, in a situation in which it seemed impossible to him that Japan might concede defeat, he reported, if all Japanese had not been killed. He therefore considered the loudspeaker messages enemy propaganda, an illusion.

4

IN A SUBURB OF DRESDEN

STORIES FROM THE BUNRAKU THEATRE

GEORGES DIDI-HUBERMAN ON THE TERM
  'MIRRORING'

IS THERE A WORLD WITH NO OEDIPUS COMPLEX?

THE CONSPIRACY OF THE 47 LOYAL MEN

In a suburb of Dresden

Under keen observation by the Stasi, an esoteric group taught and breathed in a suburb of Dresden in the early 1980s. Outwardly, the group did not violate any laws of the German Democratic Republic. They performed their civic duties and their work to perfection (albeit always with the reservation of the visions pursued by the group). The members couldn't be put behind bars. They claimed to possess secret knowledge from the 1920s, which they wanted to contribute to the new socialist reality.

The theories they set down in newsletters referred to their belief that extra-terrestrial intelligence ('from distant stars') had made two previous appearances on our planet. The first time in the far north, later moving on to the 'roof of the world'. And on another occasion, significantly earlier, ON THE JAPANESE NORTH ISLANDS. Hence, there was a type of 'connection' between Europe and the Far East. Although the second group of extra-terrestrials had been of non-Aryan nature. The East German authorities, they advised, ought to bear this 'original form of dialectic' in mind, even if they were incapable of making political use of it. According to the analysis by the relevant GDR state institution (Department of Churches), the sect could be categorized as *racialist*. It was clear that it differentiated between a preferred status of genome bearers ('extra-terrestrials', 'chosen ones', 'praecepti') and common people, whose standing merely corresponded to the French national assembly's call for fraternity.

At the time when the initial investigations into the esoteric group were conducted, the state institution was distracted by observations of radical movements within central German Protestantism. Also by the disruptive citizens who numbered themselves as members of the Catholic diaspora in Magdeburg. The officer in charge of the file on the apocalyptic sect was relocated to the border troops. One remarkable aspect was that the Dresden group did not consider itself part of the extra-terrestrial elite. It merely insisted on its KNOWLEDGE of a DIRECT RELATIONSHIP BETWEEN OUTSTANDING SPIRITUALITIES IN JAPAN AND NORTHERN EUROPE. Stasi Minister Mielke's office considered them fools, and pronounced that the GDR had to allow itself a certain basic level of such delusions. This categorization was not without ridicule. It came from minds trained in materialism.

'Most distant love'

Rather like I look back from 2017 to 1967—fifty years apart, my right hand lying idly on my desk—Master Hokusai looks with his downward-facing eyes fifty years back to the year 1793. Kabuki theatre this evening. His eyes shifted fifty years, he watches a drama. At the same time, he sees a thousand other stories in the circuit beneath his scalp. We can't rule out that this DEMON ends up WITH BLISSFULL EYEROLLS or with another part of his spiderlike mind (seen from 1843) in the Paris of 1793. There, heads are toppling into waiting baskets. Enemies of the people are executed on a production-line basis. And so Hokusai paints his series 'head of stone', though no executions took place in Edo in 1793. The surface of the pond in the garden of Prince Konoye has goose pimples in the feverish north-easterly wind constantly blowing over the island for eight weeks. Yet it would be exaggerating, says the master, to accuse the pond of sensitivity, of a feeling for that which is happening on the night side of the planet (it is afternoon in Japan). A throat capable of singing is separated from its body there by the guillotine. The prince's pond remained calm when a tremor buried 200 people under rubble in Abruzzo. The pond is an imprecise seismograph. The hand of the master, however, remains precise. The wind over Japan is deceitful. The north-easterly is regarded as constant but isn't, consisting as it does of a series of rapid gusts, resulting in an impression of evenness. Evenness would be the wrong category, also, to measure a distant disaster which sends its echoes to the Far East with a time difference of ten hours' solar position: whenever a new transport of condemned men and women is carted to the Place de la Concorde.

Four stories from the bunraku theatre

Kiyomori of the Taira Clan became lord over Japan in the year 1167 / It was his will that a temple should be completed on a certain date / The sun sank, however, before the work was ended / So he stopped the sun's path with his fan—

> DRAMA: Hirugaesu Nishiki no Tamoto
> ACTOR: Nakamura Utaemon III as Kiyomori
>
> DATE: November 1812

    ✢

Prince Atsumori of the Taira Clan was besieged in his town by the ruler Kumagai and taken prisoner / Kumugai was so touched by the young prince's beauty that he wanted to spare him / Admonished by his vassals for sparing an enemy, he must then have the prince executed after all / In another version of the drama, Kumagai saves the prince by releasing his own son for execution

> DRAMA: Keisei Homare no Sukedachi
> ACTOR: Nakamura IV
>
> DATE: January 1850

    ✢

The noble Jiraiya had become head of a band of robbers after the loss of his family / Surprised on a journey by a snowstorm, he found shelter in an old woman's hut / When he tried to murder her in the night, his sword broke and she transformed into a man who proved to be a demon named Senso Dojin / The two of them liked each other, and the demon explained spiritual secrets to Jiraiya

> DRAMA: Jiraiya Coketsu Tan
> ACTOR: Ichikawa V and Jitsukawa
>
> DATE: *c.*1854

*

General Noki Maresuke, Japan's minister of war, followed Emperor Meiji to his death when the former died in 1912. 'Death lives behind the hill on the right. I go from nothing into nothing. Why should I fear? Why should I lack loyalty?'

Heiner Müller: 'The most important thing for me in Japan, even on my first visit, was the traditional theatre, especially bunraku'

KLUGE: How long does it take to fly to Japan?

MÜLLER: I always flew via Frankfurt, then Paris, then Tokyo, then Toyama. It took 20 hours, I think. We flew over Siberia. The Siberian route is the only reason to fly to Japan every now and then. When there's no cloud cover, the view of Siberia is amazing.

KLUGE: If the operas had to leave the opera houses and become partisans, there'd be an anti-opera, a countermovement. It wouldn't necessarily involve singing. Would there be opera in the form of messages in bottles?

MÜLLER: If we're talking about Japan—the most important thing for me in Japan, even on my first visit, was the traditional theatre, especially bunraku. That's the classic marionette theatre. It's the theatre of the future. It's a *Gesamtkunstwerk*, with opera integrated into the whole, not separate. In Europe it's become an extra, arising from the illusion that we were revitalizing ancient Greek tragedy that way. In Japan, the marionettes are about three-quarters life size, made in detail, with realistic masks. Then there are puppet masters who operate the marionettes visibly on stage. They're dressed entirely in black, their faces covered in black too, with only slits for their eyes.

KLUGE: They speak to the audience?

MÜLLER: They don't say anything, they operate the marionettes. An important marionette has *three* operators, the less important *two*. The personnel has *one*. One's in charge of the right arm, the left leg. There's a platform on one side where the musicians sit. They're the actual actors, they sing and speak the dialogue. It's absolutely insane.

KLUGE: The unity of prompters and orchestra?

MÜLLER: The puppets' movements are realistic, but they're dead. Death stands behind them and moves them. On the platform are short, fat, older Japanese men. They have a lot of experience. They create the dialogue.

KLUGE: They tell stories?

MÜLLER: A performance lasts five to six hours. There are a lot of intervals. There was one scene—the daughter of a samurai has fallen pregnant to an enemy samurai. He has spurned her, as was to be expected. She comes to her parents' house, wanting to give birth at home and be taken in. The mother runs like a headless chicken—this is the marionette—between the daughter and the father and moans and groans. The daughter wails and the father yells. One singer performs these three voices, these three roles—incredibly naturalistic but also artistic. It has an enormously emotional effect, but it's completely artificial too. That's a future into which opera can be integrated.

KLUGE: The story's told separately. The elements are separated. If you applied it to *Tristan und Isolde*, without having expectations of Bayreuth in mind, how would you tell a story like that?

MÜLLER: It would be ideal if you had people to act it and people to sing it, separately.

KLUGE: You could even go without the singing. One group tells the story. An orchestra plays. In-between, the marionettes are on stage. A stage designer can operate the teaser drapes separately. The lighting can be separated too, so that light play happens. If you could control all the elements freely like this, could you tell more than always the same story?

MÜLLER: Wagner gave us an approach for doing that. But it's just that one approach. The greatest invention in Bayreuth is the invisible orchestra. It's really enormous. I almost can't stand any concert—the more advanced the music is, the more unbearable it is to see the musicians. It's the same with the singers' catalogue of gestures. They need certain gestures for their breathing and to support their vocals. That's why you never get away from that odd opera pathos. The pathos comes from the necessity to breathe properly. It's difficult to reduce that.

KLUGE: If you set up a Siberia in the middle of Richard Wagner, I mean if you create empty spaces, you only need part of the time, according to the Japanese method of separation. Maybe you keep the score as it is, but you could tell more of a story as a plot. You could add in the backstory. You wouldn't be so restricted in terms of plot. There are times in that opera when nothing happens.

MÜLLER: Almost nothing.

KLUGE: You could add in the lineage before Isolde, and the line before Tristan, and all the splinters connecting King Arthur's round table with ancient Greece. You could tell incredible amounts of variants on dramas, one after another.

MÜLLER: Bayreuth is a utopia. The genius thing about the festival is that it only happens once a year, so its time is limited. There's no repertoire. You'd have to expand it with performances lasting 24 hours. That would be the consequence.

KLUGE: The general who vanquished Napoleon and decided the Battle of Paris in 1814, that was Blücher. He was defeated in the Battle of Ligny but then he brought things to a turning point at Waterloo with his German contingents and thus temporarily hindered civilization from crossing the Rhine. How could one present him?

MÜLLER: There's that story of his imaginary pregnancy. He was lying under a horse.

KLUGE: Napoleon assaults, he comes from Elba, he's brought together about 200,000 men in troops, comes up against the Prussians first, whose approach is the fastest, set in motion by the Congress of Vienna. He attacks, breaks through the frontline, encircles them and destroys the Prussian cavalry. One of the men left lying there—his leg trapped underneath a horse—is Leberecht von Blücher. No one knows whether the leg is broken. An adjutant defends him against French dragoons, then they pull the commander out from under the horse—hydraulically in a way—like with a tractor. He groans and is rushed away on a stretcher. Gneisenau decides that night, we won't retreat, we'll follow the enemy even though we're defeated. That was the unexpected, which takes them to Belle-Alliance, to Waterloo, and seals Napoleon's fall. After that he has his phantom pregnancy, he feels violated by a corporal.

MÜLLER: He wanted to understand the defeat of Ligny, which had been denied.

KLUGE: But he *really* gets a belly full of air, a gigantic belly, and he says in French: *Je sens un éléphant là*—I'm pregnant. In confidence, he informs Wellington when the date of the birth will be. He thinks he's a woman. A Prussian general. The envoy von Schön tries desperately to get him out of the game in London—he's invited over there, as a victor. But he won't be taken out of play, he carries his belly around with him and tells people when the baby's due.

Is there a world with no Oedipus complex?

In 1904, a Japanese student of Sigmund Freud paid a visit to his revered master in Vienna. He reported from his psychoanalytic practice in Nagasaki that he had not encountered a single trace of the Oedipus complex, neither among patients from the countryside nor among sufferers from Japan's cities. No well-hidden or camouflaged remainder of drive that might have considered killing the father! Naturally, the respectful disciple did not wish to import heretical claims to Europe. He promised to go on looking and to increase the level of his attention considerably.

Did the FAMILY CONTRACT (*contrat familial*) at the basis of all human organization differ in Japan's clans from the European-Greek-Mesopotamian-Egyptian model? There may be regional differences, was Freud's polite and disinterested reply. In France, the sun, *le soleil*, was masculine, he said, whereas in the Celtic cultures of central Europe the mother star had feminine attributes.

Freud was captivated by the ghost stories from Japan his student told him about, which reminded him of 'Transylvanian stories'. It's all hearsay for me, Freud explained. Might it be possible, he asked, that his gifted disciple's protocols, attempting so hard to remain orthodox, contained a hint that the Japanese mental nature, recently so freshly and newly awakened from the Middle Ages, industrialized swiftly amid borrowings of the achievements of foreign lands, constituted a case of NEOTENY (Freud translated the word as 'juvenilization')? A culture discards its adult part and begins to transfer its experience from generation to generation via its infantile understanding.

Of the three development stages to adulthood, it omits the magical phase. Then the Far Eastern variant of the development of drives, Freud deduced, would not extend beyond animism—ghosts lie in wait in every bush. The dead are alive just behind the hill. How superficial the religious efforts, the selective use of Buddhism! Freud talked himself into a morning-time conflagration, if only to ward off the critique concealed in the disciple's comments. Freud knew the religious intermediaries or priests in Japan, referred to as *bonzes*, from the first act of the opera *Madame Butterfly*.

The Japanese disciple had a counter-myth to Oedipus to offer for Japanese conditions. He had *always* found traces of this counter-myth. Usually unconcealed. Where the father's murder ought to be awaiting discovery, he said, there was a HESITANT HERO to be found. The hero's name was Ajase. The myth had presumably arrived in Japan from India. Ajase is his mother's messenger. He is unsuited for duelling between knights (*daimyō*). He is a spirit who, when attacked by a rival, becomes a woman. He had not encountered such a spirit in the European libido, Freud said, politely rejecting the interpretation. And thus the guest's efforts to integrate a slice of Japanese experience while respecting the correct psychoanalytic theory failed due to the master's derision.

'Japanese officers' particular skill for tomfoolery during drinking sessions and entertainment programmes combined with simultaneous ability to conquer foreign countries'

When Japan occupied the German colony of Tsingtau—an outpost where an Austro-Hungarian navy battalion was also stationed—with 'the utmost insolence' in 1914, Freud returned in conversation to the visit of his Japanese disciple. Namely: if the animalist, early-childhood world view ('all things are animate') is not followed by a MAGICAL PHASE ('secret powers are acting, and my wishes are powerful spirits'), then the animist, 'innocent' tendency leaps directly to an OMNIPOTENCE FANTASY. If this is not founded on magic, there is no need for it to be scared of itself. It can be exercised without inhibi-tion and collectively. Such a fantasy of omnipotence cannot be corrected by reality.

Freud rarely expressed a conclusion directly. However, in the cafe where the conversation took place, he left it open as to whether the young Japanese nation's conspicuous lust to occupy foreign countries might have its reasons in the absence of one of the three childhood development phases. In which case, the 'rejection of *traditional* adulthood' and the 'skipping of the   magical phase' would be the foundation of a particular talent for conquering the world.

1968

Is it a consolation for antifascist theoreticians in 1934 that all Nordic heroic sagas tell of sadness?

A strange feeling here beneath the pale sun of Denmark in fresh summer air, on garden chairs and with a desk. The planes and submarines of the fascist enemy, shortly to beset England, are marked on a map. The propaganda pictures are clipped out. They are for Brecht's *War Primer*. The poet is working on it with the refugee Walter Benjamin, his guest.

On that summer's day, the two of them nourished their thumos, the imperturbable disposition, with observations on clear weaknesses of their opponents' ideology or theology. They needed consolation. Benjamin remarked on a common factor in all heroic sagas of medieval Europe. They were, he said, determined by ORIGINAL SADNESS ('mélancholie originaire'). Charlemagne failed to bring Roland back. He should never have left the rear guard at the Pyrenean pass, Brecht responded. Indeed, what was the point of the entire expedition to northern Spain? They had known from the outset that the difficult march back would follow the advance. Brecht wanted to include the episode—and examples from other heroic tales, also from the *Edda*—in his *War Primer*. To do so meant defining more clearly the term ACTS OF DESPERATION (which was how they regarded the National Socialists' behaviour). Benjamin interjected that, in his impression, every young culture of Europe displayed this tendency for 'anticipated grief'. That seemed too pathetic a formulation for Brecht. The rule of Napoleon III lasted nineteen years, then collapsed. The pathos of the imperial regime had consisted of 'administered grief': a political and general constitution of SAD PASSIONS. The two men wanted to cast such and similar words into texts that morning. Beneath a sky from which the sun did not emerge.

Notes from Georges Didi-Huberman on the term 'mirroring'

'Moses' soul reflected the divine message LIKE A CLEAR MIRROR.' 'When evil sees itself in a mirror, it recognizes its ugliness and freezes.' 'In Japan, the mirror, along with sword and jewel, is one of the three SACRED IMPERIAL TREASURES.' 'Octagonal mirror = symbol of the sun queen Amaterasu. Mirror corresponds to the number eight (Velimir Khlebnikov).' 'In *A New Year's Eve Adventure*, Erasmus Spikher sells his reflection to his beloved Giulietta and thereby loses his soul. Andrei Tarkovsky wanted to make a film out of the story, directly before his death.' 'Gaul women were buried with their mirrors, 80 BCE. In ancient Egypt, the words MIRROR and LIFE are identical.' 'The Titans, wild fellows, took Dionysus' soul prisoner in a mirror. Even though they had no practical use for the God fixed there. Look for source in Ovid!'

A puzzle for Max Weber

The course of the Russo-Japanese War from 1904 to 1905 and that of the Russian Revolution of 1905 were a puzzle to Max Weber. From that point on, he began to learn Russian. In the interest of puzzling them out, he also founded the journal *Archiv für Sozialwissenschaft und Sozialpolitik*, in which he addressed the pertinent social-science and policy issues thrown up by the year 1905, pursuing the subject until his death. How can it be, he asked himself, still in Heidelberg, that the Japanese, coming directly out of the Middle Ages, had accomplished an industrial revolution (and evidently a special form of capitalism) in the space of only one generation, in around thirty-six years, a societal transformation that had overtaken and defeated Russia? When no Reformation, no reprocessing of the Christian conscience, no secularization through bookkeeping and cohesive accounting (which requires a period of three hundred years) had prepared these Antipodeans for such development? Was his thesis of the origin of capitalism from the Protestant ethic wrong, Weber asked, or was Japan's rapid industrialization an unreality for which his theses did not apply?

Many years later, a student of Niklas Luhmann continued this intensive CAMPAIGN OF PUZZLING OUT. He had noticed a certain fixed nature in Japanese industrialism in the defeated country's post-war development. Participants in a production society could not don the capitalist character mask so exactly, he wrote, if the impulse to do so did not come from within (otherwise the contradictions, the struggles, the otherness of the root compared to the final outcome would show themselves in tiny oscillations and irregularities). The scholar spoke of an 'acting performance of an entire nation'. This was founded on a masked form of labour only found on the Japanese islands, for which a name had yet to be found. In his ZOO OF CAPI-TALIST VARIANTS, this species is at 143rd place. In terms of significance, however, the system theorist places this 'imitated capitalism of Japan' in place 3, directly after the CALVINIST PRIMORDIAL CELL at number 2.

Slaughter of heroes (*androktasia*)

At Burg Wildenstein in April 1945, in a black mood due to the course of the war, Martin Heidegger was occupied with the appearance of the KAMIKAZE PILOTS in the distant war theatre in East Asia, because a young Spanish woman had asked him about them. Though everything was in smithereens, he could still turn to the wise Swabian Hegel for information. The young pilots, their heads crowned by a white tie, upon it the morning sun, who cast themselves in their flying machines upon the inflation of ships approaching the islands of their fatherland, seemed a puzzle to the philosopher. The Spanish exchange student's question concerned a comparison with European heroes, including heroic Roland in the Pyrenees. Heidegger had not observed any such kamikaze disposition among the German holders of the Knight's Cross he knew. Present with all their fibres in battle, their senses remained concentrated on homecoming. Whence this disdain for life among the Antipodeans?

What concerned Heidegger even more: Why did such dedication, unconditionally risking life, remain so futile? The deployment of life against an American enemy, in which the biologically inherited drive for self-preservation prevailed as the main drive, hence a deployment of servants, ought to have resulted, according to Hegel, in victory.

The shooting down of youthful pilots, of ENTHUSIASTIC MEN WITH COURAGE TO FACE DEATH, like a hunter shoots a flock of birds down from the sky, seemed to him a SLAUGHTER OF MEN. The expression came from ancient Thebes and referred to the carnage of the embattled brothers

Eteocles and Polynices. They killed each other, neither victorious. The corpses of their retinue scattered around their own. It was due to their hotheadedness, to fate, not to a violation of the rules of victory as described in Hegel's *Phänomenologie des Geistes*. The image of the Japanese kamikaze pilots clearly differed from this source. For Heidegger, the essential difference seemed to lie in the LACK OF AN OPPONENT. There are not, he explained to the Spanish student, two people facing each other in this final battle, nor two parties of fighters. Instead, those fighting on both sides seem to me to belong to different worlds, like in a SHIFT OF THE WORLD, which only the gods may cause. The pilots plummet onto the American seamen pent up in the steel bodies of their warships, who cannot recognize the pilots' bravery. The sailors see lurching planes, already in flames. They hope to shoot these pieces of ore into the sea before they touch their ships. All fervour. Absence of knowledge. Around them, like smoke, the papery crackle of the press. It is not non-industrious servants and boldly attacking masters facing each other; a third thing, a laming element, swathes both sides: a BATTLE CLOUD. The pilots, Heidegger said, plummeted into a kind of cotton wool.

The MOTIVE for their willingness for sacrifice seemed even more puzzling to Heidegger than the external occurrences. He sought examples of sacrifice. The message at Marathon in Hölderlin. 'Heralds of victory come down!' They were heralds of victory, not 'luckless ravens'. In Europe's exaggerating Celtic or depressive Nordic heroic sagas, Heidegger could find as few parallels to the Japanese mental attitude of the kamikaze as in the recent months of the war. Here, there seemed to him to be a difference between the allies Germany and Japan. His laconic answer to the Spanish student: 'Our boys, our best men, are all dead.' It was up to her to find out what he meant.

The sad tale of how a father kills his son

The armourer Hildebrand, a companion to Theodoric the Great, spontaneously cut Kriemhild's throat out of indignation that she had killed Hagen as he lay tied up in his dungeon. That happened through his own will. Against his will, he killed his son, Hadubrand. On his return from the barbarian court, in an Alpine passage, the two of them met. The son in search of the father he thought lost. Why do they not recognize each other? Their approach is depressive, as though the blow of fate were determined from the outset. Hildebrand had indeed recognized Hadubrand—he had informed him he was seeking his father Hildebrand.

Hadubrand considered the aged stranger's statement that he was the armourer Hildebrand a provocation, clothed as he was in battered armour. He had a clear image in his mind of his father as he left the court many years ago. On the horse before him, a mare, sat a braggart, perhaps a supplicant hoping to deceive him. The stranger's declaring himself unwilling to fight worsened the situation. The youth drew his sword, attacking impetuously and uphill. The end is well known. The youth's corpse lies in the dust. His father hacked him to pieces in a fairly professional way. Once the fight had broken out, he too, the experienced man, could not rein in the fury of the battle—the difficulty of returning to 'nothing' when everything is agitated, the horses, the weapons, the senses. Something inside me surges ahead. The emotion does not say: I.

The old man carried out his son's burial. He did not want to lay the badly damaged corpse over his horse and arrive in Aquileja that way. He feared the questions. Nothing of what had happened should ever have taken place. And so he dug a hole there and then, in the grass and stone. He ruined his sword, not having any other tools at hand. He laid his son in the hollow. Earth over the top. At his latifundium, which he reached three days later, the servants greeted him.

Listing of heroic patterns

The bookkeeper Fred A. Friedrichs, in 1999 still employed on an unlimited contract by the Messer/Griesheim company in the Rhine-Main region, now unemployed thanks to the Internet and the Indian service economy, takes his universal notebook and notes down from Lord Raglan's THE HERO the 19 ATTRIBUTES of all heroes of Europe and Asia Minor:

(1) the hero's mother is a virgin queen

(2) the father is a king

(3) he is often a relative of the mother

(4) the circumstances of the birth are unusual

(5) he is assumed to be the son of a god

(6) attempts to kill him at his birth

(7) but he is 'spirited away' by a ghost

(8) after a victory over a giant, dragon or other monster

(9) he marries a princess

(10) becomes king

(11) there follows a period of government with no particular occurrences

(12) he grants laws

(13) later, he loses the support of the gods or his followers

(14) he loses the throne, has to leave the town

(15) this leads to a mysterious death

(16) often at the top of a mountain

(17) if he has children, they do not follow on from him

(18) his body is not buried

(19) a remembrance ceremony is held, often several

All elements of this pattern apply to the protagonist Gilgamesh of Uruk. Only a few to Hector, Gottfried von Bouillon or Caesar. Items 1, 2, 4, 5, 6, 7, 15 and 19 apply to Jesus Christ. None of the items, Fred A. Friedrichs adds, apply to Knight's Cross holders from the Second World War. The common imagination from which these attributes emerged, he writes, is not to be trusted. 'Electoral fraud without an originator.' 'Internet of the imagination.' That can be proved, since Trump.

156.8.

The white knight rode until evening

The white knight rode until evening, and came to a house surrounded by wooden battlements. He heard a maiden singing, endlessly beautiful and in a loud voice. He fell to thinking and let his horse wander where it liked. The horse was tired, having walked a long way that day. It was on a Saturday in the middle of August. He sat lost in thought, and the horse wandered into a moor dried out by the heat and veined with deep ditches. The horse was exhausted and fell into one of the ditches; then lay on top of him for a long time. His shield broke into three, and the rear of the saddle broke too. His pages helped him up with great effort. He was badly bruised and lamented a great deal. He rode on and came to a churchyard. [. . .] The history tells us Lancelot is very unhappy and languishes for the woman he loves, and for the messenger he sent to her, for the messenger should return and bring him what she has to say to him, this woman he loves more than anything in the world. He cannot enjoy pleasure or laughter and has no other joy in the world than losing himself in his thoughts. He eats and drinks and sleeps neither by day nor by night, he spends his time at the very top of the tower and looks around, as a man does who is in great misfortune. Now it happened that Sir Gawain and Sir Hector had ridden long through Sorelois, asking for Galahad, and found no news of him, when one day a maiden passed their way on the road on a handsome palfrey. Gawain greeted her, she thanked him and asked where they wanted to go. 'We cannot find what we are looking for,' said Gawain. 'What are you looking for?' 'We're looking for Galahad, dear maiden,' said Gawain, 'the lord of this land, but we can find no one to tell us anything about him.'

Debris of ancient tales in a medieval heroic story

Gawain, the 'golden-tongued'. Anselm Haverkamp points out a Shakespearean fragment in which the hero Sir Gawain is called 'a coppery oddment of the hero Ulysses'. Gawain knows how 'to place his words like Ulysses, but also to hide what he says beneath many words'. 'He lies like gold.' In Old Celtic, *neats* means WETNESS. *Neits* means HERO. Phonetically, the two are difficult to distinguish. The hero is given his tasks by his mother's brother; a maternal assignment, in other words.

Gawain fights the witches of Gloucester. He takes his ship through the mists of the Faroe Islands. He is the fourth on the left at King Arthur's round table, clockwise. He is loyal, although his wily tongue could commit betrayal at any time. Haverkamp refers to him as an 'anti-Macbeth type'. He does not find the Holy Grail but he does free a hundred imprisoned women. Only with Parsifal and Lancelot (both several places lower down the table) does he reach the Grail's mountain. Here, he seizes the sword with which John the Baptist was beheaded. The sword is kept in the vaults of Halberstadt Cathedral. Marries Florie of Syria. Their son Wigalois half Celtic, half Phoenician.

Gawain is the opponent of the Knight of the Lantern. In *The Story of the Crop Eared Dog*, he frees Alastrann the Wonderful—who has been transformed into a dog—the brother of the sorcerer who proves to be the Knight of the Lantern.

Gawain promises to help his friend Pelleas, who loves the beautiful Arcade. He pays a visit to the recalcitrant Arcade and claims to have killed Pelleas, in the hope of awakening the young woman's love. Yet he falls in love with her that same evening, and Pelleas finds the two of them lying together in the bedchamber. HE LAYS HIS SWORD BETWEEN THE SLEEPING LOVERS. The next morning, Gawain sees he has done wrong, and leads Arcade to his friend.

Rage, the organ of ancient heroes

Four voices guide the ancient hero when it comes to rage. Just as the main winds come from four directions. In the right hemisphere of the brain, the heroes hear the VOICE OF THE GODS. In the left hemisphere, the LOGICS OF THE DAY take effect: gripping a weapon, a carving knife to divide up the roasted meat. The third voice, the most powerful, results from the permanent control of the PRIDE THRESHOLD. If this threshold is crossed, a storm is unleashed in the soul. The blaze leaps up and 'has done' before the great hero even notices that he's killed the injurer of his pride. If he is to control himself, he must generally avoid situations in which this eruption might take place. The fourth voice, finally, is LUST, located more in the throat and on the skin than in the muscles or bones. The heart 'swirls around' it, it doesn't reside in the heart itself. Lust is a greedy voice that devours everything that reaches its lips. The soul of a hero never grows older than three years. It freezes and becomes part of his armour.

By the time this type of rage was replaced by the NATIONAL SOCIALIST MOVEMENT, the UNWILL OF THE NATIONAL COMRADES, the right half of the brain was already numb (ancient voice No. 1), the lust organ in the skin, diaphragm, testicles was tamed (voice 4). Few short cuts. Congestion, many voices 'like the whining of dogs' (ancient voice No. 2). The third voice, the storm, the flame, transformed into the rhythm of Otto engines.

'LEAVE PLACE, LEAVE TIME, LEAVE MOON BEHIND, /
WALK WITH NO PATH, / THUS YOU WILL FIND THE
DESERT'S TRACE.'

'SWEET EARTH, THE GOOD COW, RECEIVED THE
RICH SEED OF HEAVEN IN HER WOMB, THE SEED OF
THE HEROES WOOD AND REED'

THE CONSPIRACY OF THE 47 LOYAL MEN

Conversation with the expert on Japan, Joachim Kersten, on the most popular drama in kabuki theatre: HOW CAN A PERSON TRANSFORM HIMSELF WHEN HIS MOST IMPORTANT AIM IS AT STAKE?

KLUGE: What is a rōnin?

KERSTEN: He's a wave man, a samurai without a lord. He no longer has a master so he can't be a samurai any more. If he doesn't have that, he has nothing at all.

KLUGE: Why a wave man?

KERSTEN: Because *rō* means wave and *nin* means man. *The Forty-seven Rōnin* is a drama.

KLUGE: *The Forty-seven Loyal Men* was put on the kabuki stage in 1706?

KERSTEN: Based on events of 1701 and 1703.

KLUGE: On 21 April 1701, a provincial prince, Asano Naganori, the lord of a small feudal estate, loses control at the court. He is provoked by a powerful minister.

KERSTEN: Kira, an expert on ceremonies.

KLUGE: Asano draws his sword and injures Kira on his forehead.

KERSTEN: Why does he do that? Asano was asked to hold a ceremony, along with another daimyō. The two of them are not practiced at behaving and dressing correctly at court. They have to ask advice from the experienced Kira. But he will only give his advice if he's bribed. Without bribery, he gives false advice.

KLUGE: Nothing is more dishonourable than appearing before the prince of the land in the wrong clothing. So Kira makes a fool of Asano.

KERSTEN: Asano draws his sword in rage and injures Kira. He has drawn his sword at the court of the shōgun. His punishment is to kill himself.

KLUGE: There's a court of law and it advises the vassal who has broken the peace to commit seppuku.

KERSTEN: The court condemns him to do so, it's a penal law measure. The privilege of the samurai was merely that they were allowed to kill themselves. Asano takes his farewell from his most loyal liegeman Ōishi. They look each other in the eye for a long time. Asano kills himself. Ōishi swears eternal revenge, never to be appeased. The shōgun won't permit that, though. The normal way would have been: Kira insulted my master, my master died as a result, and now revenge is due. We will kill Kira within the next twelve months. That is reported to the shōgunate.

KLUGE: That would be allowed in principle, because Confucius considers blood revenge acceptable. A son is not obliged to live under the same sky as his father's murderer, and the closest vassal is like a son.

KERSTEN: There were originally 300 samurai whose daimyō had committed suicide. They all swore revenge. But the wheat was separated from the chaff. Forty-seven loyal men remained, others defected. The forty-seven obeyed their leader Ōishi, the forty-eighth. The blood oath was well known. The spies of Minister Kira and the shōgun were watching the group. The forty-seven transformed themselves.

They abandoned their status as knights. They fell into common neglect. They sold their belongings. They divorced their wives.

KLUGE: They were undead.

KERSTEN: They had sworn to take revenge at any price. So they needed a disguise. Drinking. Gambling. Their leader Ōishi visits whorehouses, socializes with would-be samurais. His best friend comes to him and says: It can't be true. Your father-in-law has disinherited you. One of your sisters has become the concubine of the enemy, Kira. Ōishi draws his sword and the friend draws his. Ōishi's blade is rusty. That's the final proof: a samurai who neglects his sword is no longer a samurai.

On a stormy night
the 47 rōnin
attack the
corrupt Kira

KLUGE: One night, the forty-seven rōnin come.

KERSTEN: Kira is holding a sake party and the guards are drunk. The rōnin break in. Kira is a coward, he hides in a coal-storage space. They find him and he says: I'm just Kira's highest-ranking servant. Then Ōishi says: 'Kira must have a scar on his forehead.' They check and he has the scar. Then they cut his head clean off. They take the head and hold a public procession and carry the head to their master's grave.

KLUGE: Two large parties at the shōgun's court. One would like to attack the forty-seven, the other wants to defend them under all circumstances.

KERSTEN: This act is supposed to reinstall the moral boundaries. The iron principle, allegiance, is underlined by the clever actions of the forty-seven loyal men's concealed commando operation.

KLUGE: That appeals to the shōgun.

KERSTEN: They are celebrated. We weren't wrong about you. You were clever.

KLUGE: They're captured but they are held in princely conditions until the *bakufu's* verdict. What is a bakufu?

KERSTEN: It's a shōgunate institution. It's housed in a tent. These rōnin are also heroes because they proved through their deed that Kira was a coward and a scoundrel, which is what killed him. They needed to provide that proof. It snows during the night, and that new snow in December is the symbol of the purity of their deed, the purity of strong will, the purity of the heart. That's the symbol of the white, which returns with the kamikaze pilots, the white silk scarf, the cherry blossom, the eternally ephemeral that constitutes the character.

KLUGE: The forty-seven commit sepukku. Their bodies are kept in a temple. It's a sacred shrine to this day.

'A whole world for mist.'

In his happiest times—never more than 2 metres away from his wife Aino—Christoph Schlingensief was in Iceland. It remained a mystery how he had got there from Nepal without spending much time in Germany. Everything up there is impregnated with moisture from the Atlantic, the clouds come uninterrupted. As he regarded the island primarily under the aspect of his current film shooting, he was sure the land of the sagas would remain alien to him for a long time to come. 'What I know least about, I find easiest to empathize with.'

He filmed a man with birds' heads, running on the beach. That brought about another staging: the battle of a dwarf against the 'Knight with Bird's Head'. Actually, Schlingensief should have been in Japan at that point. His invitation expired because he didn't take it up.

What was left of this plan to visit faraway Japan—an IMAGINATION CATCHER and a VACUUM OF UNDER-STANDING for him like Nepal or Iceland—was that the film material he improvised on that day, related to the *Edda* saga cycle, was influenced by 'Schlingensief's image of Japan'. Around midday, the film was most concerned with mist. The only place to film mist in nature was in the direct vicinity of the geysers. So Schlingensief ordered seven fog machines from a film equipment hire company in Copenhagen. They were to be flown in by the late afternoon.

The planing of the gods

When I was young and the world in my favour, it says in the *Apocalypse of Abraham*, I 'planed' at my father's gods.

Planing = I clean them, they are nourished, I wash their mouth openings, hear them breathing, I hone them into shape.

At the time in which my doubts had arisen, I transported a load of freshly washed gods to a newly built shrine. The wagon's axle broke. The statuettes broke into pieces. None of their powers had saved them from the fall. Nothing in them put the broken pieces back together over night. That increased my doubts. I was astute, I was interested, I wanted to have powerful gods around me. The next day, two stones that were godly fell into the water. Nothing helped them out of the pond. The blocks lay in the mud where the carp live. I still thought it possible that the gods of my father (and of my mother's brother) were only powerful in communion, as a choir, when they were together, but were weak during transport and in isolation. That was before my enlightenment. My father did not believe me. I did not dare to repeat any of my 'experiments' in front of him. I was reluctant to topple my father's gods, because I assumed then I would also make my father fall.

In the *Dialectic of Enlightenment*, Max Horkheimer and Theodor W. Adorno say that enlightenment is processed even in myths. Therefore, they teach that we should take possession of such older stories, verse by verse. In alliance with these myths, they write, there is a greater prospect of defeating the 'myth of the twentieth century' (and several of the new myths in the twenty-first century).

Spirit of departure, commodity fetish, pogroms, reality principle, mass media cannot be thrown into a lake as stone blocks. They don't splinter on the ground or sink under water. The statuettes of our times contain lightness, human strength (the light weight of the target groups gathered inside them).

Rage in the age of the machine gun

R.L. was a highly gifted woman. She crossed the Prussian–Russian border and got all the way to Amsterdam. Although she felt no affinity with the military, she had still acquired the vocabulary, the necessary imagination to include Friedrich Engels' comments on the end of the barricade in the age of the machine gun in her writings. She wrote, for example (also under the impressions of the Boer War): running with rage, spears and spirit up against the row of Winchester rifles mowing down the approaching men from a Boer laager—that is a misunderstanding of the reality of long-range weapons. Nothing, however, prevents the enraged from attacking them in their sleep at night. If the revolutionary robs the oppressor of his sleep, he annihilates him. If he stabs a sleeping man in the chest, his replacement soon arrives from Europe; if the attack is repeated from behind, from the flank, the nothingness of the Savannah, if the revolutionary abducts the machine gun and ammunition in the night, the forty-fourth replacement of the imperialist snipers (here, R.L. was deliberately conflating the Boers and their opponents, the British) will lose courage and think long and hard whether to board the ship that takes him closer to that fate or whether to, 'mutatis mutandis', leave the palisades of his farmhouse to threaten the Bantu land.

In the spring of the workers' movement

The trainees and secretaries of the Second International sat on long benches in their courses. Anarchists from Barcelona still sat alongside workers' leaders from the Ruhr region and schoolteachers from all over the Reich. Next to them economists. They copied down from the blackboard: 'Courage of knowledge', not 'rage of knowledge'. Not martyrs, *heroes* of labour. 'Furore of the uprising'. Difference: dead labour, living labour. THE STRUGGLE OF LIVING LABOUR, ITS FIGHT FOR THE REAPPROPRIATION OF DEAD LABOUR (OF MACHINERY) AND ITS CONNECTION TO THE HUMAN SPIRIT. Drop by drop, the human spirit flows out of the machine, but it is a spring tide of performed labour that flows back out of the factories into humanity in the end. Is this comparable to an ocean or a continent? Learn to swim if the boat has a leak. How can I know the 'cowardice of thought' before it spoils all deeds?

24.Ⅲ.0

156点.

Hokusai and the cross on the skull top

As is well known, Japan has more active ghosts than Europe, where they have been aggressively decimated since the eighteenth century. Hokusai refers to the skull with a cross on one side of its crown as a 'Western rarity'. It is, he claims, the mask of a Spaniard. The Netherlands waged an eighty-year war against ghosts like this. It was for their sake that the British fleet was founded. Rather than that, Hokusai says, one must take care of ghosts. One should, he says with the anticipating gaze upon the view he will have when he reaches the age of 170, cultivate ghosts for Europe out of Far Eastern cuttings, and return them to the wild there. Only good ghosts, bearers of wisdom and wit, are of use against the GHOST OF MODERN MASS MOBILIZATION, be it consumerist or populist.

5

CHIMES OF THE GLOBE

FROM THE JŌGAN TSUNAMI IN THE YEAR 869
TO THE TŌHOKU QUAKE IN MARCH 2011

PRIMORDIAL FRIENDS OF NUCLEAR ENERGY

Cosmic music

The chime of the earthquake that shifted Japan's North Island 4 metres to the east could be measured as far away as the Swiss Alps. The entire globe received its pulse. These are—according to Johannes Kepler—the chords of Planet Earth. Some of the notes follow one another at an interval of a thousand years, and have a slightly different sound when they are repeated. Others come at briefer intervals. The RESIDUAL RISK (inaudible of itself) can be heard indirectly, so Kepler's claim, because it reacts in the manner of an APHONIC WALL. While there is only *one* WARNING PORTENT with recorded wording, such BLINDSPOTS OF PERCEPTION are countless: chimes of the globe.

A residual risk

On 11 March 2011, when reports of an earthquake reached Europe from Japan, the fate of a hotel restaurant was decided on the MONTE GENEROSO in southern Ticino. From this Alpine restaurant, guests who arrive at the hotel's 1650-metre altitude via cable car can savour a view far across Italy's lowlands, over coffee served only in pots. The limestone beneath the hotel's terrace contains some seventy caves, some of them dating back to the Ice Age. These hollow spaces might lead to the hotel's foundations collapsing; they had already caused cracks and made the building subside by 10 centimetres. Supporting pillars proved to be crooked. The mountain emitted long creaks and groans. A provisional wooden viewing tower was promptly opened up as an alternative tourist destination next to the cable-car line. The hotel and restaurant were closed.

Now, however, geologists and structural engineers have written an assessment report, establishing that the RESIDUAL RISK is actually minor. The building, they judge, might slide slightly further but it would not reach the edge of the mountainside. They recommend banning overnight stays in the hotel but allowing visitors to enjoy the view again from April. They may be served refreshments, as long as they don't dance.

15.6.13.

In the Mariana Trench, the atoms can cool for all eternity

Dr Sigi Maurer, a Swiss man in the service of the Japanese television channel NHK, held an opinion with little majority appeal. He maintained that the crumbling and contaminated material to be removed in Fukushima (or to be covered over with a sarcophagus) should be taken where the catastrophe had started: to the depths of the MARIANA TRENCH, the earth's deepest oceanic indentation, slightly southeast of Japan. The SPOIL should be poured into the trench. After the fading of the last half-lives, it would eventually turn to sand, stone or even water, even though humankind would no longer exist by that point. Would that not risk the life on the bottom of the trench, a mysterious biotope, unique on the planet? Dr Maurer was asked.

Dr Maurer responded with a remark on DIMENSIONAL RATIOS. Compared to the enormous mass of water that the trench to the southeast of the Japanese isles contained, the nuclear material to be deposited there was insignificant, he said. Something else would have to apply, he admitted, for humankind to have the idea of disposing of the nuclear waste there (instead of in unsafe salt mines). One had to be prepared to sacrifice something, though, he added, when it came to providing humankind with energy at the lowest possible prices. Grief was always concerned with sacrifice. As, however, the deepest depths of the ocean were unfamiliar to humankind (or to readers, listeners, media users), they would hardly grieve for what they didn't know. We only grieve for what we love. In the case of the unknown, however, we can only *imagine* we regret its disappearance.

24.11.0

15.6.8.

Treasures of the deep sea

In the deep-sea trenches off Japan, mats of rare archaea are found on the sunken bones of drowned whales. Ten years pass before such a skeleton collapses, pressed upon by the water pressure resting on it, and preserved in this way as though under a second skin. The bacteria, which do not exist outside of the deep sea, can produce seven new species in this time. A large US washing powder company is using submarines to search for this COATING, for use in producing a special low-temperature cleaning agent. TREASURES OF THE DEEP SEA.

Evacuating the capital

Twelve high-ranking officials, none of them responsible for the issue, had come together for a meeting in the 37-million-inhabitant city of Tokyo. The defence minister was one of them. In the week after the Fukushima disaster, it depended on the hand of God, or on the mysterious will of powerful ancestors, whether the wind turned to the south. Then the radioactive cloud would reach the capital. Some 37 million people (and that is only a statistical estimate, which does not reflect the actual concentration of inhabitants at individual locations) cannot be housed in any one other place in Japan, said the head of the waterworks. Should we attempt to evacuate by dividing them between many prefectures? Putting them in sports halls or swiftly erected tent cities? There aren't that many sports halls and tents in the whole country. Have any calculations been made? asked the imaginative director of the finance ministry which has central authority over corporate tax for all Japan.

The problem of mass groups is that we can only deal with such large dimensions of people with the aid of the vessels in which they are organized: boroughs, neighbourhoods, precincts, busloads. Without place, time and impetus for motion (which the individual's free will determines consistently), the mass is abstract. Ungovernable? Or not even existent? No, it is highly substantial, but still unreal. What do we understand unreal to mean? With no place in this world.

Like monstrous worms, the columns of vehicles and evacuees would block every exit on the outward roads, said the defence minister. The 260-kilometre metro tunnel and its raised lines were just as unsuitable as evacuation routes, as they would quickly become blocked, added the financial expert. We must avoid such a mass exit at all cost! And bans or a news blackout would be pointless undertakings. One needs an alternative evacuation route to block an evacuation route. The head of the office for insurance handbooks knew that from reports on the Second World War.

Due to the radioactive disturbance, there was little to see

In the pocket of the thick protective suit of one of the BRAVE MEN who had temporarily left the centre of Fukushima's nuclear power station and then returned and managed to adjust the controls before being fatally contaminated, there had been a primitive digital image-recording device. The size of the palm of a hand. The engineer had put it on the desk next to him and switched it on. It contained the only moving images from the inner circle of the damaged command centre. The military detachment leader who later found it and initially intended to hand it over to the power station company (which wanted to keep the information secret, however) backed up his find by copying the video.

The device's automatic focus system, without initial instructions and thus reacting uncertainly, had switched between long shots and close-ups, later superimposing both recording perspectives in an anarchic sequence. It resembled videos made by a Mars robot. The small camera maintained its position as its owner had placed it. At one point, a brief gas explosion. The colour modulator was intact. So this was how a disaster looked on the ground.

Neither dawn nor dusk could be seen from this room strictly isolated from the outside world. Not immediately comprehensible, the video information lasted a period of 17 hours. The miniature device had an extraordinary battery life. Had all elements in place to prevent a mega-accident been as capable as the dying hero, the owner of the recording device and the reliable device itself, the disaster would have been averted from the outset. Only the plutonium-contaminated Reactor No. 3 would have remained a serious problem.

Men prepared to die wait in the right place

The technicians who maintained their position (replaced every hour) in the control room and in the pumping station of the cooling systems were referred to as 'workers'. They were not working at that point, because nothing they did (and they knew it) would have any effect. They weren't WORKING, they were HOPING—that the high-voltage power would soon be connected, driven on fervently by other technicians. Only then could the cooling cycles begin to 'work', and they would see by their technical stutters, their malfunctions, the exit of steam and energy, where to make repairs. They kept their labour available, similar to a fortress defending itself, as a reserve at this key control centre. This WAITING PREPARED TO DIE IN THE RIGHT PLACE is part of the understanding of 'work in the emphatic sense', according to Prof. Bert Haseloff of Harvard. Material-altering influence, when exerted by humans, Haseloff maintains, is based on a subjective-objective standpoint and not on any individual action.

Haseloff points out that Heidegger assumed there was 'the hand' for humans (in the brain, in the body, in nature, in social relations) and not two hands. The hand was the principle of the entire developed body and mind. Thus, there was only ever *one* dedication to death or *one* courage in the face of death and not two of them. Before the 'last assignment', he maintained, the singular and the plural became mere phrases.

The electrician

He was the fourteenth-ranking technician responsible for the nuclear power station's electricity. All thirteen of his superiors had run away. He had entered the zone poisoned by elementary particles and turned off all the electricity. He could not condone a conventional accident caused by burnt-out electricity cables happening on top of the nuclear disaster. The damage this hero of responsibility sustained to his intestines, mucous membranes, skin, brain and nerves (not including his spermatic cords) was irreparable. He did not have to pay a visit to the works doctor to know that, and the doctor had fled the scene some time ago. For a brief while, it seemed possible that the energy company's press department might take possession of the brave electrician as a public example of willingness for duty. Then, however, the bearers of partial responsibility for the department began to consider any public appearance counterproductive for the company. They concentrated their efforts on making the company forgotten. Depression had seized all hierarchies.

What had the reason been for his dedication, the doomed man was asked. The man listed all the risks posed by high-voltage cables in a shattered nuclear power station no longer under human control. He described the branches of the electricity cables, which were by no means fully recorded in the emergency plans.

'I would not have liked myself if I were sitting down some-where now, rescued, and eating food.' Some of the cables were attached to the base of the water tank. He said he'd had to swim. The reading on his meter had varied strongly in the water. Then the indicator had stayed put at the top of the scale. My entire graduating class, the technician said, was recruited from university to this reactor. We were welcomed with great respect. I behaved as was expected of me. By the company, but above all by my comrades. His mouth was swollen, his vocal chords signalling impending disobedience, as he said: It conforms to the technical guidelines. He meant not their wording, but their meaning. When he spoke of comrades, he was talking about imaginary companions, as there was no one but him on site. 'I carry them with me in my head.'

26.11.0

The leader of the swimming team

The Takata High School swimming team was seen marching to the municipal open-air pool, a kilometre away from the school grounds. From the edge of the pool above the broad sandy beach, there was a view of Hirota Bay. Passers-by watched the column turning onto the path to the swimming pool. That was the last time the young people were seen.

The town of Rikuzentakata has 23,000 inhabitants. Some 2,300 have been missing since the tsunami. Around 9,200 are living in evacuee camps set up in sports halls and tents. Since 1820, the number of pupils at Japanese schools has constituted the same percentage as in Germany and France. Since the Meiji Reform, state schools have been at the centre of local communities in the prefectures and towns. What the temple once signified is now embodied by the school: a piece of pride. Now, Takata High School is the largest evacuation centre. A delivery truck drives into the schoolyard. The drivers show the corpse of a student from the neighbouring town of Ofunato. There were fifteen minutes available for the tsunami warning. It took five minutes for the news to spread among those responsible.

Rikuzentakata is a fishing town extending from the coast into a valley and up to the hills behind it. The 257 students in the school building were led up the hill behind the premises. The school swimming coach, Ms Motoko Mori, one of the missing people, was last seen running towards the pool. She is said to have tried to bring back the swimming team under her care. It is said she took the children to an indoor pool that was built so that the expected water masses could flow through the building between stilts. She wanted to rescue the children onto this 'island'. Nothing of the building was left intact.

Pictures of missing people are pinned to the walls of the high-school rooms used to house evacuees. Mounty Dixon, a journalist from Anchorage (Alaska), believes he observed parents and relatives of the missing clinging to fantasies that their children are still fighting for their lives out there in the now calm sea. There are also islands far out beyond the bay. A group of relatives pooled their money to equip a motorboat to check the islands. As Dixon reports, the Japanese widely believe in ghosts, including good spirits that lead children back to their parents, against all probability.

The fishing town once possessed a coastline with a thousand conifers. The surrounding hills are now dotted with a garland of shipwrecks. In the school centre, the talk is of 1,700 missing persons. The word 'missing' is a euphemism in this case, Dixon writes. There is one positive piece of news, however. An eighty-year-old woman and her grandson survived, trapped in the basement of their flattened house, by eating the contents of their fridge. The thin boy crawled through the rubble towards a light that proved to be the day.

3.VIII 15

Future perfect tense in Fukushima

The water pumped into the sea from the reactor's contaminated cooling tanks will take twenty years to sink to the bottom. During all that time, it will travel as droplets. The ruin of Fukushima, however, will still be radiating in 100,000 years' time. In several years, it might be demolished. Then there would be hand-sized chunks of cement and metal, suitable for transporting in containers. Only—transporting to where? How much uninhabited territory and how many underground caves do the Japanese Isles have at their disposal? The company responsible, even now merely administering its future mountain of debt, possesses no means to purchase such rare land. It will no longer exist in a few years' time. New brave experiments with untamed forces of nature will occupy the chroniclers of the next ten years. None of the responsible cadre will have committed seppuku.

Primordial friends of nuclear energy

During the burial of nuclear waste in one of Australia's deserts, in the depths of which an ancient mountain range is found (dating back to the time when the planet was forming), researchers accompanying the progress of the nuclear waste disposal like good bookkeepers came across a remarkable phenomenon. The treasure of nuclear waste had evidently awakened achaeobacteria trapped in the rock of the prehistoric mountains to new life, though it was previously considered extinct. Across a distance of 60 kilometres, the bacteria had migrated through the rock to the waste deposits in only two years. They had penetrated or eaten through the concrete sheath of the depot and the protective steel-and-copper containers beneath it, only to reach the energy source on which they had once thrived in the earth's core (when that source was even stronger in the stone). Now they had settled in the nuclear waste, developing an unstoppable life force. The researchers wondered whether they would multiply without measure once they reached the attractor. That did not seem to be the case. Connected to their familiar energy source, in other words sated, they remained in place.

Nature magazine rejected the researchers' article. The editors objected to the thesis that the archaeobacteria had migrated a distance of 60 kilometres. How were the researchers to know that the objects they had discovered in the mountains deep underground as quasi-dead material and then found again as radioactivity eaters in the nuclear waste were the same microbes? They would have to study the phenomenon further.

The consequences of the discovery had also been insufficiently studied, the editors remarked. It was possible, wrote one of the peer reviewers on whose vote publication in *Nature* depends, that the old greed might break out anew after the exhaustion of the nuclear source where the guests had settled, selection might set in within the evidently mutated community and these high-risk life forms, contaminated as they were, might start wandering the land again, attracted by power stations with constructed defence lines incapable of deterring them, if only enough of them turned up outside these fortresses.

Happiness as a through station

Small fish cannot live in the large saltwater deserts. Thus, a pair of fishes had settled in the shell of a large snail on the edge of the shelf, living happily in this housing until the 2011 seaquake. Then the calcium carbonate shell was torn apart. Its debris was washed kilometres away. The two fishes 'withered and died'.

It was under similar circumstances that my parents, brought together more by coincidence than by necessity, set up home at No. 42, Kaiserstrasse. They could not have built or fitted out a house like that themselves (the society capable of that had passed by them long before and was now lost and gone). They lived in the house on loan, so to speak, until the tectonics of events—in their minds—drove them apart. They both died at a moment when a life as they wished to live it was practically out of the question (even a life in borrowed buildings). Should they walk the earth again, which I dearly hope, they would no doubt have a rather confused view of conditions. It is not certain whether they would find an abandoned shell or another form of housing for themselves.

3, VIII 095

'We fly through the night'

The entire globe. The stars circling around it. As a globe, the earth looks benevolent. The planet produced us, says Hokusai with a precisely pointing finger, but the earth hasn't decided for good whether it wants to have us.

The references preserved in Mesopotamian texts (Gilgamesh, Old Testament) to a flood that almost destroyed humankind—legends that don't exist in Japan—are deceptive in that they claim natural disasters require a divine order. This error is based on a failure to recognize the autonomous will of the cosmos (almost all of it too hot or too cold for human skin), in other words, the normal mode of nature. Our ability for illusion protects our senses from the paralysis that would strike us if we were to look CRUEL NATURE directly in the eye. In Japan, the swiftly changing winds that drive fast clouds ahead of them help matters. There is little to see of the cold stars.

Hokusai compares us illusion artists with children who close their eyes in the face of danger. 'I'm not here.' 'My name is nobody.' 'What I am is home and dry.'

In a museum in Paris in 1889, a visitor looks at the oil painting *The Raft of the Medusa*. The situation, says Hokusai, is unreal. In truth, the visitor was once on the warship that sank, and is (if he was lucky) now on board the raft. It takes another case of good luck for the visitor to be depicted in the painting as one of the few survivors. Such a NEW ROBINSON CRUSOE STORY would be about REPAIR EXPERIENCE ON THE SAILBOAT OR RAFT. Before arrival at the cliffs of the desert island.

O God! what cruel distress
as the desolate barking of the wild storms
howls about us though fog-filled air
We fly through the night.

6

WHERE IS THE INDEX FINGER OF HOKUSAI'S
  RIGHT HAND POINTING?

THE ADVANTAGE OF MISUNDERSTANDINGS

PURE RAGE IS A CONCENTRATE

UNSUITABILITY OF RAGE FOR REVOLUTION

'ALL HORIZONS HAVE WINGS'

'SOLDIER, REST! THY WARFARE O'ER'

The eagle

The talons, often falsely interpreted by laymen as 'feet' when an eagle 'stands' on branches or steep ridges, are grippers of prey. Talons are flight aids. Baselitz draws them as two bars placed like a V. Next to them a thick stroke. Thus, they appear like a Roman six or like the symbol on the uniform of a lance corporal. None of the eagles' talons remain the same in these sketches, however. 'Lapsing to its knees'? 'Lapsing to irrelevance'? Disoriented as a bird that can't fly and is told to 'stand up'? The Japanese master was eighty-three years old when these eagles were produced. The eagle blue against a pale blue background. Elegant.

With ultimate elegance, a General Staff man boarded a Fieseler Storch in April 1945. A plane capable of flying so slowly and so low through the night that no enemy hunter can spot it. The flying stagecoach was to take the officer, the emissary of Alfred Jodl, to Pilsen. Would it have been possible to get the Dönitz government, the last of the Reich, from Mürwik to the Bohemian Protectorate? Safety for a few days? A nest near the Alps for the commanders of the Reich? With a wooden leg (the original was lost at Kharkov), a new type with every promotion, the major boarded the passenger seat in the two-seater plane.

Where is the index finger of Hokusai's right hand pointing?

What about the master's left hand? It points downwards. In other sketches, it has vanished in the spider's web. THE FINGER OF THE RIGHT HAND, however, which otherwise helps him to draw, is pointing to the West, where the sun stays awake when it gets dark in Japan. Each finger differs from the others. The eyes also differ: buttons, seals, two barques, funnels, gorges, cores, windows, cellars. But they always consist of several ghosts. The stumps of teeth ridicule us. Once I'm a hundred and ten years old, the man intends to say, every dot and stroke from my hand will lead its own life. That was in 1859, three years before the birth of my paternal grandmother.

The advantage of misunderstandings

I am one of Georges Didi-Huberman's assistants. I'm helping set up his exhibition in the Louvre. It's about the continuation of Aby Warburg's Mnemosyne Atlas in the twenty-first century. Being French, I have to feel my way into much of it first.

My right eye is disabled by a skin growth. A thin layer of skin stretches across the lens, inoperable. My eye registers imprecisely. I read in the catalogue (partly because it's in italics and small print): A GREAT MIGHT DOWN THE DRAIN. In fact, I see in the picture something like the tip of a rocket. The left ear hanging from the ghost's head seems overly large to me. Like that of St Jerome 'in his study, listening to a dove'. That was how I wrote my commentary on the picture. But the picture was called A GREAT NIGHT DOWN THE DRAIN. I refuse to rewrite my commentary just because of a misunderstanding.

'Nature turns a blind eye'

The exploring hands of an experienced midwife have found an anomaly. The uterus is kidney-shaped. The embryo of 'crooked wood'—human, that is—can well adapt to its crooked incarceration. The drawing (see page 196) is inspired by a work from Leonardo da Vinci's collection. Such a birth cavity may (across six generations) produce a Duce Mussolini or a working-class activist in a Turin car factory. Be it bent or rounded, it makes no difference. Only linear comes to nothing. The uterus can't be a stroke or a line. That's what's causing the pleased expression on Hokusai's old face. Look at the nonchalance with which his left hand is placed, the mocking slant to his shoulders. As long as there are midwives, wit exists on the human level. Two fingers of Hokusai's pointing hand point downwards. That's where Peru is.

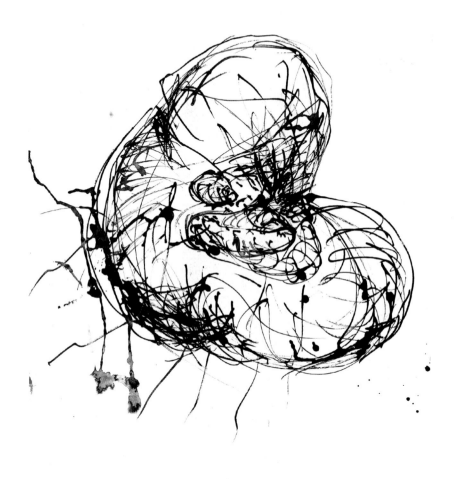

3. VIII 075

A determined woman

The wife and later widow of the fourteenth ruler of Japan was called Jingū-kōgō. Deities had ordered the ruler to conquer the kingdom of Silla. The tennō doubted the messages were genuine, however, consisting merely of a voice in the right half of his brain. The deities' rage led to the ruler's sudden death, upon which the imperial widow took charge of the troops and conquered the land of Silla in a three-year military campaign. During this time, she delayed the birth of her son by using stones to block her uterus.

How do heroes come about?

Very few heroes observe their deeds while they perform them. They are made heroes by non-heroes who watch their battles and declare them their role models. In some cases, women have set their sons on the career path of a hero through a bundle of expectations.

A well-known historian in California—still appalled by the Third Reich's Nordic propaganda—intended to take a hard stance on the HERO BUSINESS. He critically reconstructed the lives and deeds of alleged heroes. Then, though, he fell in love with some of them, and his publication turned out quite different to what he'd planned.

In the writer's basements

Ernst Jünger, a lifelong soldier, kept a special collection of insects in glass cases in a basement room of his house: ENRAGED WASPS, pinned down just like all the creatures the writer possessed, but their armour toxic yellow in colour—still full of WRATH. With the rage of such wasps, if one could direct it, one might have been able to change the outcome of the Battle of Flanders in 1914, as these flying creatures, comparable to a squadron of horseflies, could have crossed water and swamps to attack the British trenches and empty them of enemy soldiers. The French flank open, breakfast on the Champs-Élysées.

THE COUNTERPOLE OF RAGE IS ANTI-RAGE,
A RAGE-DESTROYING ANTI-COURAGE,
NOT A GENTLE DISPOSITION.

g.XII.6.B

Unforgivable deeds

Insane with rage, Patroclus fell asleep and was stabbed to death by Hector. Like a FIRE GOD OF RAGING, Achilles. He attacks Hector and drags his corpse, chained to his battle chariot, around the walls and gates of Troy. Until this day. Too late did he recognize his terrible mistake, the seal of his own death.

'Like a tornado touching down / The dream selects its sleeper'

At the snack bar next to the metal factory, he ate a hot sausage. After that, no more for his digestive system until his death. After 'a hard day's work' he climbs down from the truck before all eyes. From a suburb of the federal capital on regional trains to the Netherlands, from there to France and to Italy. On foot, the long walk from Milan's main station to the station concourse of the industrial suburb where he is shot dead.

Rage of a Celt

A Celtic hero was known for the fact that, when the rage blazed within him, 'his blood leapt up as high as the mast'. That's a physical state that can only be maintained for long in stories. The blood circulates as a fountain for a few minutes. Then it has to return to its bodily grotto. The hole in the skull closes up.

'Brightly blazing rage'

The CEO of a major corporation made his position untenable
with an act of rage. A school student and two friends smashed
up a classroom and destroyed the school's biological collection,
kept in a glass cabinet. He then stoically accepted his expulsion.
A sociologist established that something like a wave of rage
spread across towns in the Swabian Alb during 2016, after
several companies went bust and closed down. The rage of a
hundred thousand, endemic, appeared like a disease, altering in
the space of weeks into MOROSITY: war inside the souls. This
bitterness, the sociologist posited, had transformed into IRE,
then to OBDURACY. Skin rashes. Passivity. No longer voting
in elections. No dancing. Few words. Pick-me-up pills prescribed
by the doctor were no use at all. But where, the sociologist
asked, had the original rage gone? Not a trace to be found.

4.170

15/18.

Destinies of rage

In large parts of Poland, Galicia and the Baltic, writes the French historian Fernand Braudel, the peasants were successively dispossessed by a decentrally organized aristocracy during a century-long process. Instead of wheat, one could harvest rage from the fields. It was 'altering rage', in that the resulting rural exodus took resources away from the aristocracy and thus prepared the division of Poland between Russia, Prussia and Austro-Hungary. The NEWLY ENRAGED IMMIGRANTS (most of them from the ruling class that had formerly betrayed the peasants), who fled to France after Russian troops defeated the Polish uprising, were not wanted by that country's liberal monarchy. They became the starting point for the foundation of the Foreign Legion. Drainage of the enraged to Africa. Rage, Tocqueville writes, can only be imprisoned, obliterated or exported. A quantum of Polish courage, mixed with Irish, Swiss and high spirits from circles of déclassés, was involved in the legion's invasion of Syria, which brought calamity over the country in 1850. Moslem attacks on Christian churches were revenged by destruction of whole towns. That was the origin of the misery in and around Aleppo today.

THE JAPANESE ARE MASKED WHEN THEY APPEAR
AS IMPERIALISTS AND CAPITALISTS. IN TRUTH THEY
ARE ALWAYS ANTIPODEANS. LEARNING FROM THE
THOUSAND MASKS OF MASTER HOKUSAI MEANS
LEARNING TO BE HAPPY WITHOUT VICTORY.

Colours of rage

Hokusai gives rage the colour white. In Germany, we speak of a 'red blush of rage'. In a novella, we can read 'pale with rage'. 'Black with rage.' No one, however, says 'blue rage'. 'Beige-snow-coloured-radish-blue to green with rage' is an uncommon phrase. Crimson or scarlet would be possible, however. According to the Halberstadt physician Dr Eicke, all rage colours, when visible in the face, are bad for the circulation.

Pure rage is a concentrate

A merchant had taken in a child suffering the plague from the side of the road (his coach had already left the danger zone), lost his own child as a result and adopted the foundling in its place. This young stranger grew up full of wilfulness and peculiarities and, enabled by the merchant's good nature, threw his adoptive parents out of the house. His benefactor's rage grew so great that he killed the 'alumnus', the 'rescued child', and—condemned as a murderer—refused penance, so as to surely end up in hell after his execution, where he hoped to continue exerting his rage on the adopted child until HIS absolute destruction. This severity of temper, PALE RAGE, is something few people can summon up, and those few cannot maintain it over long periods of time.

23.ᵥₗₗ₀₁₅

History of rage

The routine exerciser of violence, Agamemnon, is ranked slightly higher than Achilles, the son of a goddess. This different ranking programmes their conflict. On the surface, it is a matter of a female slave and a captured weapon. In truth, their argument is rooted in the question of primacy in taking the spoils.

The hero Achilles is so physically gripped by rage that he falls mute. For days, weeks. The archaeologist Luca Giuliani points out that an Athenian tragedy presented the SPEECH-LESS RAGE OF ACHILLES in such a way that the Athenians saw only a man on the stage for half a day, squatting soundlessly and deedlessly with a blanket over his head. That is said to have caused great TENSION in the audience. The next day, a declaration of war against the city of Argos.

With the Greeks' best warrior waiting motionlessly outside the camp at Troy, the Trojans make a push forward. They will soon reach the Greek ships and burn them. Achilles' companion Patroclus disguises himself in his friend's armour. As an ACTOR OF HIS GREAT FRIEND, he seeks to scare the Trojans. His stiff movements (and his avoidance of confrontation) mean the enemy easily spot the imitation. The violent rage, the battle-altering thumos of his role model, shining like an aura, is missing. The armour stops Patroclus from breathing and he is struck dead by Hector, the idol of the Trojans. The armour is pulled off his body on the battlefield. Stained with blood, the naked man lies on the ground. Once again, the 'threshold of pride' is violated for Achilles. The wind of rage turns from Agamemnon in a new direction: Hector.

Before gods favouring the Trojans could whisper counter-commands in his ear or curb the weight of his deeds, thus faster than the voice sounds in the hero's head, Achilles has torn down the counter-hero Hector. He wrests Patroclus' armour (which once belonged to him) from the dead man's hands, he demolishes the corpse and throws it underneath the couch on which he—only the fourth trumpet, the sensual language of saliva in his mouth, allays something of his previous rage—has lain down for a triumphant feast 'like a ruler from Asia'. Then, in the last chapter of the *Iliad*, Hector's father, the ancient Priam, close to death, approaches the landlord of rage as he dines. The king has crept past the guards. He enters the tent with a gesture of humility. A dangerous moment! One false word, one misinterpreted motion, and the voices of rage, either in Priam or in Achilles, might break out in unison, compelling a fight. It would be decided swiftly—a catastrophe for Achilles if he were to kill the old man. Yet also misfortunate for the king (with regard to his intention of recovering his dead son), if he were to use a hesitation on the hero's part to pierce his ribs, driven equally by rage.

'Those skating on thin ice will only make it if they skate as fast as possible.' The two protagonists of this final chapter in the epos about rage did just that. Over the course of the evening, they reconciled. Achilles, who had no father, took the old man in his father's place for a short time. And King Priam took the hero in his arms like a son, both knowing how soon he would die. The stations of the proceedings are depicted on Athenian amphorae. Luca Giuliani does not assume that the two men's internal FEELINGS or VOICES had abated in the course of the

15.6.3.

events. The enlightenment work of myth, he says, lies rather in a kind of gained ability to distinguish, in RECOGNITION. Both men became 'hollow creatures'. Each moves into the other's gap, his lack, his hollow.

A text by Hegel on 'master and slave'

The daring Swabian philosopher Hegel, in his youth—when he still formulated in an unbroken forward-moving direction, before his betrayal of his lover and the betrayal of the son he had conceived with her out of wedlock ripped up his soul and rendered him toothless in the end—never used the word 'hero'. For hero, he used the term 'master'. The master could choose 'whether to dull his mind in lust or die in battle.' In both cases, he would not remain a MASTER in the long term. In that respect, the philosopher continued, 'MASTERY is an impasse'. Hegel had in mind the abdication of the agrarian aristocracy, who had been masters over Europe for eight hundred years. The rise of bourgeois societies troubled Hegel by its lack of 'heroes'. All that remained was the young. In the Lützow Free Corps: Theodor Körner, among the hussars: Major von Schill. Was 'soldier' the new bridging god between peasants, bourgeois and the young? As *homo novus*, a 'new fellow'?

The 'slaves' (Hegel used the word synonymously for workers, craftsmen) tried hard. Cheated out of mastery, they nursed—as in charcoal burners' huts—their rage. In RAGE HOUSES, a kind of barn of the soul, they hoarded a RAGE CAPITAL in writing and pictures, a subjective societal crowbar.

The setting of a border or boundary
is always the crossing of that border

Do enraged fighters and thus heroes of the modern day come more from this working side? Reading his regular newspaper, the EDINBURGH REVIEW, Hegel followed the later course of the only slave uprising ever to be successful, in Haiti.

What were the prospects? These enforced immigrants to an island who were suddenly masters? If something is missing after all, because there are now only masters and no one will work? Hegel was perplexed.

Another of Hegel's formulations

'That is to say that Man—at his origin—is always Master or Slave; and that true Man can exist only where there is a Master and a Slave. (If they are to be human, they must be at least two in number.)' On the post-revolutionary Republic of Cuba, the French philosopher Onfray writes that the punishment for revolution is isolation. The island became a Robinson Crusoe, he writes, but lacks a Friday. There always have to be two to survive on an island.

THE RAGE OF ALL OPPRESSED AND BETRAYED
HOUSES OUGHT TO SUFFICE TO OVERTURN
ALL PREVIOUS REALITY IN ONE BLOW AND
TO CREATE THE NEW MAN. RAGE SPEAKS:
I AM, I WAS, I SHALL BE.

Debate on the aging of words

The 'firebrand of Berkeley' (that was in 1968), now seventy-eight and grown slightly calmer, a leftist still roaring with vigour, wandered the offices of Silicon Valley, divided from Berkeley by nothing but a stretch of water. In search of errors for him, the scholar of the lantern, to correct. One of the leading young people in the innovation village, a great-grandchild of the flower children, had said the word German word Held (*hero*) and the German word *Zorn* were OUTDATED. It would be better to speak of hate, anger, daring or better: openness to risk—those were more modern terms. The scholar, wanting to rescue at least the expression 'heiliger Zorn' from the young man's contempt, spent a whole morning on the debate.

– The English word for the German word 'Zorn', he said, was 'wrath'.

– And here in the *Oxford Dictionary Unabridged* (the young man had called up the entry with one click) it says 'wrath— old fashioned expression or formal'. Only usable in the figurative or antiquated sense.

– But the feeling remains the same, doesn't it?

– Only in the Latin word 'ira'. (This too, the young man had looked up with three clicks.)

– And what do you think of 'bile' (*galliger Zorn*)?

– Nothing at all. Not even as a sensation.

– What about 'choler'? That would be *Koller, Wut*.

– I'd recommend that, but not for *Zorn*.

– And 'ire'?

– That would be *Jähzorn*.

– 'Rage' or 'fury'?

The young man from Silicon Valley could live with those two words. He and the scholar had one thing in common—they had both been Bernie Sanders supporters. He was also impressed by the older man's tenacity. But the advocate of progress did not accept his compromise. Both words were more like *Wut*, he answered. Similar in terms of stirrings, but not of the same depth as ZORN. THERE IS NO ENGLISH WORD FOR ZORN. When the emotion is old, why should the word for it be young? The young man, a leader in Silicon Valley, refused to enter into more fundamental debate. One can rule the world, he said, through PLATFORMS, through TECHNOLOGY or through power over CONTENT (that is: control over words), but never through all three estates at the same time. For his group, he therefore fundamentally renounced *content*. He was regarded as a successful man.

'Charisma of the drunken elephant'

We know of Max Weber that he occasionally sought the truth not in the facts but in language. An inspiring choice of words prompts clarity of vision. This experience applied to his theory of the CHARISMA OF THE DRUNKEN ELEPHANT.

He had never studied an elephant close up. He had noticed a report in a London newspaper explaining that certain herbs started fermenting in the bellies of the large creatures, in the intestines coiled within. This shot of alcohol apparently makes elephants go wild, and 'it must be a wonderful sight', he read, when they forged ahead with no regard to any hindrance. Weber assumed that likewise, confident women who lived for a long time under their husbands' subjugation (perhaps over generations, like in an elephant's belly), built up a strong sense of rage: a wrath that they pass on to their sons. Usually to the second or last-born son.

This 'inborn' courage or pride, the wildness that is initially related to no heroic characteristic and is also found in ugly men, is recognized by the pent-up hate, IN THE MENTAL INTESTINE OF MILLIONS, IN THE PROCESS OF FERMENTATION, who are no longer willing to stand their oppression. The sudden drunkenness, the charisma of their role model, seems contagious and seizes the masses who now see the smaller man, ripping up trees as a charismatic pachyderm, as their leader. With the light of a million eyes, he becomes radiant.

There could be a major difference, Weber adds, between appearance and reality in the case of such drunkenness. A later disciple of Weber's in Harvard went as far as to apply the sociological term 'charisma of the drunken elephant' to

'Donald Trump, acting out like a drunk behind Hillary Clinton's back on a TV set'. Weber had used Regional Director General Hugenberg as an example of a charismatic character, a man he had met during the war in East Prussia, but who later—four yards away from Hitler on his appointment as Reich chancellor—appeared unauthorized and useless in that setting. No wild outbreaks, no powerful presence, no uprooting trees. He had a seat in the new government's cabinet room, newly installed in the Reich Chancellery's Führer building, specially made chairs bearing the state insignia, but rarely got to take that seat. Charismatic mastery is chaotic. Like elephants running wild with alcohol in their bellies. Not exertable at tables.

Master Hokusai mocking (every) seizure of power.

Puzzles of the world spirit

Just as the voice of the earth expresses itself in slowly flowing magma, yet simultaneously in lashed-down hotspots that do not shift for millions of years (all this has its specific sound), the world spirit moves in (albeit immaterial) rivers and is yet fixed at certain points which can be tracked down by science. The fixed and the movable are scattered across all geographical areas and at the same time interlinked: rather like the springs of the Black Forest exactly mirror the leaping waters in the West of Japan's North Island. In this way, the hundred stories told by a nurse that Master Hokusai published contain the same generosity and swirl curve as the operatic performances of Bellini's *I puritani e i cavalieri* and Jacques Fromental Halévy's *La juive*, staged only a month apart in the Paris of 1835. Two torrents against intolerance. Although in Edo at that time there was no need to react to the terror of the Great French Revolution, the stupor of the subsequent reaction era, Christian fanaticism or genocide in the colonies, as a cheerful merchant class was cultivating goldfish and courtesans to satisfy its lusts in the isolated country, Hokusai's pictures are full of grief, corresponding to the sentiments in Paris at the same time. That is one of the puzzles of the world spirit, its not-yet-fully-understood geology.

'Soldier, rest! Thy warfare o'er'

Georg Baselitz's picture of a soldier, the double of a picture to be seen in an exhibition in Munich's Haus der Kunst, shows a beaten warrior. Full of grief, one hand rests on his testicles which look relatively large. Just as their representation in the man's brain, compared to that of his hands and feet (seen from an everyday perspective) takes up a disproportionate amount of space. No warrior or fighter is merely MAN. A section of chest protrudes from his uniform. Parts of his innards stored in his helmet. All this too complex to be commanded.

A brown quiff of hair escapes from beneath his head covering. Voltaire wore a bonnet similar to this soldier's. In such an outfit, Voltaire declared war on nature under the impression of the Lisbon earthquake. That was in 1755, five years before Master Hokusai's birth.

Brother Voltaire, 'that mocking Presocratic'.

Acknowledgements

I owe thanks to my longstanding editor Wolfgang Kaußen, far beyond the office of editing, for key navigational pointers to Peter Sloterdijk's Theory of Rage and the image of the hero in medieval epic literature. Many thanks also to Detlev Gretenkort for his creative balance between pictures and texts.

Alexander Kluge

Image credits

All reproduced works by Georg Baselitz from the series *Besuch von Hokusai*, 2015–2016, ink and watercolour on handmade paper, diptychs, approx. 66 × 51 cm per sheet. © Georg Baselitz 2017.

Photography: Jochen Littkemann, Berlin

Lithography: farbanalyse, Cologne